646.435

Published by Cappiello + Chabrowe, Inc.
220 Central Park South
New York, NY 10019
ISBN 0-9648720-0-5

Table Of Contents

ACKNOWLEDGEMENTS

Rather than going through an "Oscar Awards" litany, thanking my forebears, descendants, neighbors, et. al., for their help in putting this book together, I will instead, for brevity's sake, thank my husband, Tony, for his patience, support and stamina all these months, and Terry Chabrowe, my computer and marketing wizard for his guidance, advice and copy. And, most of all, my beloved customers for their help and encouragement; whatever success I may achieve always starts with them.

Foreword

I opened The Shirt Store's doors for business for the first time on May 15, 1987, with a firm idea of what I wanted it to be — a U. S. designer, manufacturer and retailer of men's 100% cotton shirts, dedicated to quality in both product and customer service. I would offer my customers variety in fabrics, collar styles, and sizes at reasonable prices. If we could live up to our motto of "Affordable Excellence," then customer satisfaction would surely follow.

As we celebrate our Eighth Anniversary, it is safe to say that we have achieved our original goals. Today, The Shirt Store has more than 15,000 customers, and those customers have helped us achieve sales increases every year — even through the recession. Why do these customers keep coming back? Maybe it's our wide selection (70 different sizes, from 14 x 32 to 18$\frac{1}{2}$ x 37), collar styles (seven) and fabrics; maybe it's the way we taper shirts for customers who want a closer fit (we don't do the easier darts that most stores do – we actually open the seams and taper the entire shirt); maybe it's services such as changing collars and cuffs on aging garments (sometimes a different label). In short, we believe that we have to do what it takes to satisfy our customers.

From day one, we've tried to be trendsetters, not followers. We have designed and produced our own distinctive line, and in the process have given the customer choices in ready-made shirts that had previously been available only to the "custom" shopper. For example, we pioneered the "Gekko," a horizontal striped shirt, and have brought the rounded spread "Riley" collar into the traditional wardrobe by offering it in basic fabrics and in a wide size range.

We also offer full-custom-made shirts that are second to none in quality and craftsmanship. Starting with an individualized paper pattern, we take it to sample for further adjustment, and then to final garment.

Our Mail Order Division is off to a flying start, sending customers swatches of fabrics which are available in their individual sizes.

We also wholesale to other stores, especially smaller retail operations which, on their own, could not afford the quality of shirt that The Shirt Store manufactures.

And we've just launched two new marketing programs. The first is our Basic Dozen subscription service. It provides a way for our customers to be sure they always have the basic shirts they need, at even greater savings, and without ever having to place an order or come into the store. The second, our Shirt of the Month Club, brings an even wider variety of styles and fabrics to our customers, at really substantial savings. Limited to the finest quality fabrics, it makes a great gift.

Finally, we have established a Broadway "connection," having manufactured shirts for the Broadway shows *Grand Hotel, The Will Roger's Follies, Penn and Teller, Carousel, An Inspector Calls, The Phantom of The Opera, A Christmas Carol, Sunset Boulevard, Show Boat,* and *Victor/Victoria.*

All this in just eight years — and our price range for fine cotton shirts is still the lowest in town: $37.50 to $87.50.

With this book, I wish to give my all-important item of clothing — the shirt — its fair recognition, and make my all-important consumer knowledgeable so that he can put his best shirt forward in his business and social environments.

Introduction

When that important meeting is on the schedule, you find yourself spending a fair amount of time — and what seems to be an unfair amount of money — on the essentials of your business wardrobe. You've found just the right suit, shoes and accessories — even the right briefcase. Now, you're at that meeting. You're all seated around the table. Take a look around. What do you see? Suits? Shoes? No. You see faces and shirts.

It's interesting that the piece of clothing that most people buy as an afterthought is the piece of clothing that other people actually see the most. Interesting, and also a bit frustrating to me, since shirts are my business.

You see, I started a business on the simple (some thought simple-minded) assumption that if I paid a lot of attention to the much-neglected shirt, eventually I'd have a number of loyal customers who share my enthusiasm for this couple of yards of cotton, handful of buttons and two collar stays.

And it's possible you may be one of them. That's why I'd like to tell you a little bit about shirts - their history, how we make them, how you should choose them, how you should take care of them, and about the only material we'd even consider making them out of: pure cotton. We'll even teach you how to accessorize them with ties, cuff links, suits, etc.

So spend a few minutes reading about shirts. (After all, you'll probably spend at least 100,000 hours wearing them.) Because once you know about what goes into a truly fine shirt, you just might want to get into one yourself.

Shirt Power

During his business career, the average man will buy at least 500 shirts, spending more than $20,000. And if you have your shirts laundered, you can add another $15,000 or so. That's a sizable investment; and one which, if used wisely, can pay big dividends.

In our society, and particularly in business, appearances do count. The better-dressed man makes a better first impression. And a better first impression can go a long way.

> *"Elegance is concentrated in the shirt."*
> —Oscar Wilde

The well-dressed man is the man in control. Being poorly dressed can take you out of the competition before you begin and leave the control in the hands of others.

A tastefully-chosen shirt and tie will help project the image of an executive who cares about presentation and details. Careful shirt wardrobing can stretch a small clothing budget and make a man look like he has made it even while he is still getting there.

Your shirt should subtly reflect who and what you are, as part of a whole ensemble that says "this is a well dressed man, listen to him." The ability to make this kind of an impact is not innate, it is learned. So, let's begin.

History of Shirts

We have no idea which of our prehistoric ancestors first cut a hole in a skin, thrust his head through it and shouted "Eureka, I have a shirt!" But we do know that this is how shirts were worn until the late 1800's, when shirts that opened down the front were introduced.

At that time, shirts, with their high, starched white collars and cuffs were more than an item of apparel. They were also a mark of class distinction. Only those who did not do manual labor—"white-collar workers"— or the landed gentry, business owners, and royalty, were in a position to wear these white collars and cuffs. Quite simply, their day-to-day activities did not get them dirty and, when they did, they could afford to have them laundered.

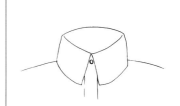

The high, starched collar

From then on, the history of shirts becomes primarily the history of collar styles. It is the most important element of the shirt, the one first noticed, the one that gives a shirt its character and, not surprisingly, it is the one that has undergone the most change.

Legend has it that sometime in the 1820's a Mrs. Montague of Troy, New York, cut her husband's collar from his shirt, washed it, and reattached it with strings. In one fell swoop she had cut her laundry load in half, created the detachable collar, and sent her husband into the world with the cleanest collar on the dirtiest shirt in Troy. And she certainly started a trend. In fact, the detachable collar is still in use today, primarily in formalwear. In the 1900's these collars were made of every conceivable material, including paper, cloth and celluloid, and all had one characteristic in common — starch, as much as the material could hold, transforming them into a form of self-torture. A soft attached collar was available then, but the "macho men" of that era scorned the wimpy comfortable soft collar and suffered in dumb silence. One particularly popular style was the stiffly starched lay-down collar popularized by the newspaper serial character Buster Brown in the early 1900's.

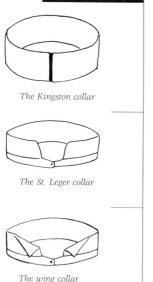

The Kingston collar

The St. Leger collar

The wing collar

The wing collar, as we know it today, is a direct descendant of these early stand-up collars. It was a standing collar with pointed turned-back tabs, and was worn for formal day or evening dress beginning in the 1880's. It is still in fashion for formalwear today. We can say that the wing collar was the first phase of the lay-down collars.

Sometime in the early 1920's, an unsung hero threw away his instrument of torture and replaced it with a soft attached collar, starting a veritable fashion avalanche, as his long-suffering brothers followed suit. White collars and cuffs had also lost some of their luster and were being replaced by shirts with matching collars and cuffs. In a short time, men's shirt fashions went from one basic collar style to a huge selection of lay-down collars, some outlandish and short-lived, but others which endure today. The process of fusing the collars (the use of a specially prepared interlining which is laminated to the outer layers of the collar to eliminate wilting and shrinking), was started in the 1920's. This process is still used today on finely made stock shirts.

The pinned or eyelet collar was most popular during the late 20's and early 30's. The pin pierced the fabric, pulling the wings of the collar together, raising the tie. Later, a collar bar was substituted for the pin. Simply clipped or slid on the edges of the collar, the bar pulled the collar together in the same manner. Its offshoot, the tab collar, became popular in the late 20's, using tabs that fasten under the tie with a brass stud to lift the tie. This style has proved to be remarkably resilient, enjoying resurgences in the 30's, in the 60's and again in the 90's.

Slotted collars were invented by putting slots on the underside of the collar to hold tiny celluloid collar stiffeners (today's plastic collar stays), which kept the collar in shape.

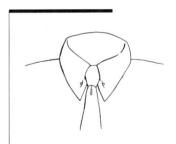

The eyelet collar

The button-down collar (a style in which the two collar points are held in place by small buttons) was developed by necessity, rather than as a fashion statement, in the early 1900's. It seems that the landed gentry in England found the flopping of collars during polo matches a "damnable nuisance" and decided to "button them down" to get them out of the way. In the process they created one of the most pop-

The Barrymore collar

ular and enduring of collars. It was rediscovered in the early 30's and has been in vogue ever since.

Straight collars have been with us since the 20's and caused little excitement from one year to the next. The only changes they underwent were dull lengthenings or shortenings of the col-

lar. The longest collar was the "Barrymore," named for the actor, who wore his points 4$\frac{1}{2}$" to 5" long. The most popular length in the 20's and 30's was 3 to 3$\frac{1}{4}$" which is the most popular length once again today.

Enamored as the fashion world has always been of all things English, it's not surprising that the spread collar was created to accommodate the Duke of Windsor's thick tie knot, the Windsor knot of the same name. When the Duke wore a tab collar on a visit to the U.S., it became the rage.

The club, or rounded, collar, inspired by the starched

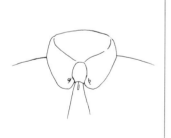

The club collar

white linen, wide, lay-down collar with round corners worn by the Eton school-boys, also became popular in the 30's.

The 40's meant war time. That meant men in uniforms. Consequently, men's fashion changes were minimal.

The 50's brought the lower-slope, short-er, more comfortable and conservative

collars into popularity—but the basic collar styles of the 30's and 40's stayed, especially straights, spreads, modified-spreads, tabs, eyelets and button-downs.

The 60's saw the "JFK" look of modified-spread collars come into popularity. Again the public took on the look of a popular leader — this time an American.

High, long and spread collars were in vogue in the 70's, as were tapered, brightly colored shirts.

The 80's brought back the shorter and more conservative looks of the 50's. The white collar and cuff was back, using both solids and patterns which complemented the contrast.

Today's collar styles are, historically speaking, moderate. The 3 to 3¼" point is again popular and styles are classic: button-downs, straights, spreads and tabs are all in style. Freedom of fashion for men is the newest trend for the 90's. Conservatism is giving way to fashion in the office. Men have more options in their dress code, especially with shirts and ties. The still-popular gray and blue suits are being joined by earth tones and, in addition to the always correct blues and whites, the wardrobe is being enhanced with shirts in greens, lavenders, pinks and creams. Stripes have become multi-colored as well as one color on white. French cuffs are increasingly popular and contrasting collars and cuffs are going strong. Collar variety is being used to give a suit a fresh look, even with a basic white shirt wardrobe.

As many of our customers have learned, a man can add new life to a suit simply by changing the style and/or color of his shirt. The shirtmaker's challenge today is to satisfy the customer's wish for a varied selection. Today's man is demanding options!

Today's Collar Styles

It's interesting to note that although collars have run the gamut from longer to shorter, more spread or less, we have always come back to the basics. It seems that collar fashions have become a small microcosm of our lives... we always return to the tried and true, the comfortable, the familiar.

The Button-Down Collar

In this most comfortable of all the collar styles, the two collar points are held in place by small buttons. It is made with

The Button-Down Collar

a soft lining and no collar stays. Usually it is styled with a soft roll and a ½" tie space to accommodate a tie easily. The collar is usually quarter stitched (the classic collar finishing), and is usually done with button cuffs rather than the dressier French cuffs.

It is usually found on more casual body patterns, with pleated backs or sleeves, rather than the split-yoke of the non-button-down styles. In many cases it is worn open for casual wear. It also looks great with a bow tie.

Although it is acceptable business garb, it should not be worn with dressy suits or double-breasted styled jackets.

It should, however, be part of the "Basic Dozen" in every man's wardrobe (page 76).

The Straight Collar

Also called the "classic collar," this usually has a point length of about 3", stay pockets and quarter-stitching. The tie space is currently about ¼" because today ties are tapered in shape, so the knots are not too wide. As in all non-button-down shirts, a heavier lining is preferred in this collar to help it maintain its shape.

The Straight Collar

This is the tried-and-true collar style. It is perfect for the job interview, the workplace, or most social occasions — and it looks good on most men.

This collar style can also be worn with a tie bar that slides on the collar and holds the points down around the tie. It looks great with a bow tie, as well as open at the neck without a tie. In short, it is the one indispensable collar style. It is definitely part of the "Basic Dozen" in every man's wardrobe (page 76).

The Modified-Spread Collar

The collar has become increasingly popular as men have added variety to their collection of collar styles. It is easy to wear, simply because of its spread.

The Modified-Spread Collar

It is comfortable on the big or small man — it will not fight the chest of the big man, nor is the spread so wide that it would be unflattering to a small man. It is the most comfortable of the non-button-down collars. Adding to its popularity, it can also be worn open at the neck without a tie.

Usually the point length is 3", has stay pockets and the collar is quarter stitched. The tie space is currently about $\frac{1}{4}$" because today ties are tapered in shape, making for a narrower knot.

The spread is such that the tie knot hides the band of the collar (similar to the straight collar) and thus even the most conservative of men can feel comfortable.

It is definitely part of the "Basic Dozen" in every man's wardrobe (page 76).

The Spread Collar

Both large and small knots are fine with the spread collar. Remember, the band of the collar is designed to show

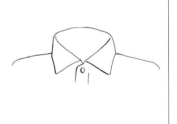

The Spread Collar

around the knot. You don't have to hide the band and use a Full-Windsor knot.

It is usually done with a higher band than the modified-spread, which makes it great for men with average or long necks, but the shorter-necked man should avoid this style — he'll look uncomfortable wearing it, even if he feels fine.

Usually the point length is 3", has stay pockets and the collar is quarter-stitched. The tie space is currently no wider than $\frac{1}{4}$", and because the spread is so wide, most knots have no difficulty in fitting.

It is considered "fashion-forward" even though the style has been around for a long time. This is probably because it is not found in the conservative dresser's wardrobe. This collar can also be worn without a tie for the casual look.

The Tab Collar

The tab collar has once again returned to the forefront of men's fashion and is being worn by the conservative button-down wearer, as well as the fashion-forward spread collar consumer.

The Tab Collar

The reason for the tab collar's appeal is simple. It gives the wearer a clean, classic look which is designed to focus attention on the tie.

It fits high on the neck with a small loop attached to both points which is fastened across under the tie to hold the points down. It is featured with many types of closures — buttons, snaps and studs. We make ours with the stud closure because it pushes the tie knot forward and arches it, while the loops keep it in place throughout the day.

Because it is made with a higher band, the shorter-necked man will look and feel uncomfortable in this style.

We prefer the point length at $2^{1}/_{2}''$, so that it does not bend up at the tips when worn. The collar is quarter-stitched, and the tie space should be $^{1}/_{2}''$ to $^{3}/_{4}''$ to accommodate the tie knot.

Stay pockets are put in the collar so that it can be worn with collar stays to give it a stiffer look, or with them removed for a soft touch.

The proper choice of fabric will make the "tab" appropriate with either a business suit or sport jacket. For the ultimate in elegance, a broadcloth fabric with a French cuff is unsurpassed. This collar must be worn with a tie.

19

The Shirt Store's Own Contributions
The "A" Collar

A take-off on the straight collar but more fashion-forward. Named for its shape, it is styled with no tie space, 3+" points, stay pockets, and edge-stitching.

The "A" Collar

The collar is made with a low band so that it sits low on the neck and frames the tie. It is a comfortable collar because it is low, and has lasted in popularity for over five years, making it a staple in The Shirt Store line.

This collar is comfortable dressed up or down, depending on the fabric chosen or cuff style used.

This collar style can also we worn with a tie bar that slides on the collar and holds the collar points down around the tie. With its collar stays removed, and worn open, it has a comfortable, casual look.

The "Riley" Collar

Inspired by the basketball coach of the same name, the "Riley" is a comfortable low-rise collar that sits into the chest and frames the tie with spread, curved 3" points, stay pockets, and classic styling with quarter-stitching.

It is a comfortable collar because it is low. It has lasted in popularity for over five years, making it another staple in The Shirt Store line.

The "Riley" Collar

This collar is considered dressy and is usually made with French cuffs, and under no circumstances should it be worn open without a tie.

The Still Popular Contrasting White Collars

The contrasting white collar is an English style that has gained increased acceptance in the United States during the 90's. It has also become very popular in continental Europe.

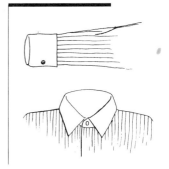

Last year, 25% of the non-white shirts we sold had contrasting white collars and cuffs. The three most popular collar styles were modified-spread, classic (straight) and tab. They have increased in popularity as office dress codes have loosened and have given the man in the office an almost infinite variety of choices.

We see more and more white collars on television, both on our media stars and politicians. Once a popular anchorman wears a white collar (or any other style), it seems to give it legitimacy and wide acceptance in the marketplace.

Some men wear white collars because they feel that they always look fresh and smart. Others wear them because they can add more color to their wardrobe while still being perceived as conservative dressers, since the first thing you see is the white collar.

I like them in my shirt line because it gives me an opportunity to introduce bold and exciting new fabrics which, without the white collar, might be too much for my relatively conservative customer base. These shirts are usually perceived as dressy and most often made with a white French cuff.

Collarless Shirts

The collarless shirt is, for the most part, unacceptable in most offices, even on casual days. This accounts for the popularity of dress shirts that can be worn with or without a tie, with traditional business suits, as well as casual slacks and loafers. For our purposes, we will concentrate on the shirts that can be worn with a suit and tie.

It should be noted that this collarless look, if desired, can be achieved by removing the collar leaf from any of the collar styles mentioned.

Which Collar is Right For You?

When deciding on a collar style, don't start with what you like. Start with the length of your neck. (Remember, the most important thing about a shirt is how it looks to other people when you're wearing it.)

The man with an average neck can wear any of the collar styles, choosing the ones he is most comfortable with.

If your neck is very short, you must make sure that the height of the collar is not too high for your neck or you will crunch the sides of the collar, making yourself very uncomfortable in the process. The modified-spread, the "A" and the "Riley" are the lowest sloped of the collars. They are also scooped on the sides, which will help eliminate the crunched collar. The tab and the full-spread collar with higher bands should not be a choice for the short-necked man. An exception to this rule is the older man with a very wrinkled neck. He might choose the high collar to hide the wrinkles and improve his overall appearance.

If your neck is very long, you will look best in the spreads and tabs. Classics and button-downs will also serve you well.

It has been said that the short man must not wear spreads because they will make him appear shorter, and the very tall man must not wear straight collars because they will make him look longer. I don't agree. The collar style will not change your height. If it looks good on your neck, you can wear it!

Cuff and Sleeve Styles

Cuffs began to appear outside the jacket sleeve back in the 1500's, when little ruffles first began to peek out from the edge of the coat. From that time on it has always been fashionable to show about 1/2" of cuff outside your jacket sleeve. Showing less than 1/2" suggests a lack of fashion consciousness, or that the shirt was a hand-me-down.

Cuffs should fit closely around the wrist so that they do not ride up when the jacket is put on.

Barrel (button) or French cuffs are personal style decisions, except in formalwear where the French cuff is the only proper finish. The sleeve length should be the same whether you are wearing button or French cuffs — you should be showing the same amount of cuff outside your jacket.

The opening just above the cuff on a sleeve is called the placket. The length of the placket is usually about 6".

Most fine stock shirts have a button on the placket so that it will not gap and show skin. In custom shirts, we find that many men prefer to eliminate this button because they forget to button it or it is often crunched by the laundry. I think the only time it should be eliminated is on the French cuff, which is turned out by design, and makes the placket button unnecessary.

The history of the placket button is found in English tailoring. The opening was referred to as the gauntlet, and the gauntlet button was placed there to enable men to fold back their cuffs while washing their hands.

The Barrel or Button Cuff

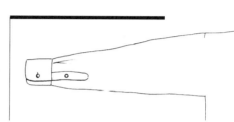

This cuff is fastened with one or two buttons and is the most common style today. They are easy to wear, less expensive to make, and are appropriate for any occasion except a formal one. They are usually done in a $2^3/_4$" width, are quarter-stitched or edge-stitched to match the collar and are lined to keep their shape.

The French Cuff

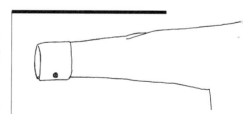

The French cuff is the dressiest and most elegant of cuff finishes. It is usually 6" wide and is folded back, has no buttons, and must be fastened with cuff links. They are quarter-stitched or edge-stitched to match the collar and are lined to keep their shape.

The use of the cuff link helps make this cuff finish even dressier. It is always worn on formal occasions and is usually seen with suits rather than sport jackets.

This cuff style has increased tremendously in popularity in recent years. It seems that men are enjoying being "dressed-up" even in these "dress-down" times. More and more men, when in a suit and tie, are choosing to go all the way and finish off the outfit with the dress cuff — the French cuff and cuff links.

Short Sleeves

If your first objective is to feel cooler during the summer, short sleeves have a definite place in your wardrobe.

If, however, you wish to be dressed properly for the office or any social occasion, do not add the short-sleeved shirt to your wardrobe. It is generally not accepted in a business environment, nor is it considered appropriate for the special dinner engagement.

Proper dress for the office, the courts, fine restaurants and the theater does not change with the temperature.

Save your short sleeves for the beach or tennis club!

Why Cotton?

It's really quite simple. No other fabric looks like cotton, no other fabric feels like cotton, and no other fabric wears like cotton.

Cotton Incorporated, who coined the trademark phrase "The Fabric of Our Lives," explains cotton's superiority in terms of four characteristics: softness, breathability, absorbency and durability.

Sometimes we do wear other fabrics, but for day in, day out good looks and comfort, nothing comes close to King Cotton.

It provides all the characteristics we want. Cotton has a naturally textured surface that seems to get softer with each use. Cotton breathes — it's cooler in the summer and warmer in the winter. Cotton has absorbency qualities that lift the moisture from the skin and up into the air. It is receptive to fabric treatments such as dyeing, and it retains color beautifully. Its interlocking fibers give it strength and durability, and with proper care it will last a long time while maintaining its original luster.

Why wear anything else?

Origin

Cotton is the soft, fibrous substance covering the seeds of the cotton plant. Its substance is pure cellulose.

When you think of cotton, you probably think of the

South, and with good reason. The Southern states of the U.S. are still among the most productive cotton-growing areas in the entire world.

Cotton cultivation, however, is far older than the United States. The place it all started, so far as we can tell, was India. In the 5th century B.C., the Greek historian Herodotus, after a trip to India, told stories of natives who made cloth from fleece that came from plants. After wending its way through India and on into Persia, cotton first made its way into Western civilization the same way that quite a few other Asiatic discoveries did — via the returning troops of Alexander the Great in about 325 B.C.

And, while we may think of cotton as an everyday fabric, it certainly wasn't back then. The fabric was immediately prized for its strength, durability, versatility and luxurious look and feel. Because of the difficulty involved in its manufacture, it was among the most expensive of all textiles, and remained so for quite a long time.

It wasn't until English manufacturers took advantage of the techniques made possible by the Industrial Revolution that cotton really came into the widespread popularity it enjoys today.

Different types of cotton have different fiber lengths. The longer-fibered cloths are usually considered the best cottons.

Types of Cotton and Cotton Terms

(Special thanks here to Gerald Varley of Vartest Laboratories in New York City, who has helped us make this sometimes confusing subject a little clearer.)

American Upland is the world's most popular variety. Originally developed in the South, it can now be found anywhere cotton is cultivated. Fiber length runs from $^3/_4$" to 1". This cotton is used in less expensive shirtings because it has a shorter staple, which spins into heavier yarns.

Broadcloth is a general term for fine, smooth cotton fabric used in making shirts. It is a tightly woven fabric with a very light crosswise rib, similar to poplin, but finer. Broadcloth fabrics are used in dress and formal shirts.

The term broadcloth comes from the use of wide looms to make fine fabrics which were of similar construction to ribbons produced on narrow looms.

Chambray is a cotton shirting fabric with a frosted effect produced by weaving white warp threads lengthwise with dyed ones (usually blue) crosswise or in the filling direction.

Egyptian Cotton is a long staple cotton, fine and silky, and is usually found in ultra-fine broadcloth dress shirts. Primarily produced in Egypt, it is now grown in many parts of the world. Fiber staple length averages $1^3/_4$".

End-on-End is a madras cotton in one color with a frosted or muted effect produced by weaving together white "end" (or lengthwise) threads with pastel-colored crosswise ones; the result is similar to chambray. Again, the most popular color used is blue.

Long Staple cotton is the professional term for the natural length of the fiber, which ranges from $1^1/_4$" to $2^1/_4$". The longer the staple length of cotton, the stronger and more luxurious it will eventually become when woven in the form of a shirting fabric. Pima, Egyptian and Sea Island are the cottons with the longest staple lengths.

The finer the yarn, the more difficult and expensive it is to make. The manufacturing process includes a process called combing, which removes all fibers below $1/2$" in length. There are many yarns used in shirting fabrics, but the finest qualities are plied together to make a two-ply yarn.

Oxford Cloth conjures up visions of old, ivy-covered buildings, and professors in rumpled, comfortable button-down shirts. Quite appropriate, too, because most of those shirts are oxfords.

An oxford is a cotton shirting fabric with a small basket-weave surface. It has a full texture. It is soft and comfortable, and usually comes in white, pastel shades, or colored stripes on white. Less lustrous than broadcloth and considered less formal, it is nevertheless one of the most popular shirting fabrics.

Single-ply Oxford is usually done in button-down styles. This heavy, beefy cotton is able to take more abuse than the lighter, finer weaves. This is why it has the reputation of being taken by the wife to be used as a nightshirt when the husband is done with it. When she is through, she will turn it over to the children to be used as a smock for art class. It gets softer and softer as it gets older.

Pinpoint is two-ply oxford. It is dressier than single-ply and usually is done in 80's two-ply fabric.

French Oxford, another two-ply oxford, is sometimes called a pinpoint with a weave. The weave resembles the pattern of pique used on formal shirts. It is silkier than solid pinpoint and, depending on the style of collar and cuff, can be dressed up or down.

All oxfords will wear faster at the friction points (collars and cuffs) than broadcloths.

Piece dyeing applies color to woven fabric and converts it from its colorless "greige" state after scouring. Finishing follows, which stabilizes the fabric and minimizes the amount of residual shrinkage in the fabric. Singeing and mercerizing can be included in the finishing process to give a lustrous appearance and silky feel to fine cotton fabrics.

Pima cotton is a high-grade, very strong medium-staple cotton developed in Pima County, Arizona, and used for fine broadcloth shirts. It is now woven all over the world. It is characterized by long silky fibers, ranging to $1^{1}/_{2}$" in length.

Pique is fabric woven into a waffle-weave. It is usually used in formal attire.

Plying is the process by which two yarns, after they are spun, are twisted together before weaving.

Single-ply refers to a weave of two single yarns. For example, a "50 singles" fabric is woven from one-ply 50's yarn.

"Two by one" or "two on one" (or 2 x 1) refers to the weave of a single yarn with two yarns that have been plied together.

"Two by two" (or 2 x 2) refers to the weave of two plied yarns. For example, "2 x 2 100's" means that both warp (lengthwise yarns) and weft or filling (crosswise yarns) are two-ply 100's yarn. Another way of describing this is "two-ply both ways."

Plying of yarn

31

Sea Island Cotton is the finest long-staple cotton, found in top-quality shirtings. It once came only from Sea Island and other islands off the Georgia and South Carolina coast, but it's now grown in the Caribbean and other regions of the world. Staple length can be $1\frac{1}{2}"$ to $2\frac{1}{4}"$. Usually this is made into combed two-ply yarn in very high thread counts.

Thread count is the number of threads per square inch. The higher the thread count, the finer the cloth.

Voile is a fine, high-twist, plain, open-mesh-weave cotton cloth. A crisp fabric of great strength for its weight. Popular in the hot summer months and for evening wear.

Yarn dyeing applies color to spun yarns or threads before they are woven into fabric. Most fine shirtings are yarn-dyed. Yarn-dyed fabrics tend to hold color better than piece-dyed fabrics.

Yarn size is based on the number of yards of yarn per pound in units of 840 yards. For example, 50's singles will have 42,000 yards per pound; 100's singles will have 84,000 yards per pound.

Choosing the Right Fabric

Before making your next shirt purchase, touch the fabric carefully. The "hand," or feel, of the fabric should be the most important factor determining your choice. Each of the weaves has its own qualities and everyone has his own preferences. The smooth, silky feel of the broadcloths, the softer heavier qualities of the oxfords, the open texture of the end-on-end — each has its adherents.

It is not always the most expensive weave that will satisfy you. For example, if you like your shirt crisp and starched, you will not like the more expensive Sea Island weaves. They are too tightly woven to hold the starch. They are meant to be soft and silky. They will also wrinkle the most.

Because of their heavier yarns, oxfords will become stiffer than broadcloths when starched. The single-ply oxford, with its beefy weight, will be the stiffest of all. Broadcloths will also starch well, if they are not as tight as the Sea Islands, and they will still remain lighter in feel and silkier in hand.

The oxfords are also less translucent than broadcloths. This feature guides many men in deciding on oxfords, especially in a white shirt, because it hides chest hair and undershirts.

Broadcloths are much dressier than oxfords. They are acceptable in most business and social environments.

Broadcloths stripes and patterns are much crisper in color than the oxfords. In oxfords, the cross-weave of color in the cloth always diminishes the color of even the deepest stripe. If you are still in doubt, buy one of each and test them. After wearing and laundering, you'll find the cottons that are just right for you.

For a well-rounded wardrobe, you'll need a combination of fabrics so that you will be able to change the look of your suit and, therefore, expand your wardrobe quite inexpensively.

Wrinkles

Wrinkles — we all hate them. We pay lots of money to take them off our clothes; even more to take them off our faces. And those darn cotton shirts just seem to wrinkle almost as soon as you put them on in the morning. Isn't that terrible? No, actually that's quite good. The wrinkles in a fine cotton shirt are a natural quality of the fabric. They're a result of the same properties that make cotton look and feel so good. So, remember, when you're in a room full of people all dressed in white shirts and ties, it's quite easy to find the well-dressed (and quite possibly the real decision-making) men in the group... they're the ones with the wrinkles.

Caring for
your Cotton Shirt

Your shirts should be laundered after each use. Perspiration and the aluminum chlorides found in antiperspirants can weaken the fibers of a shirt if left in contact with the fabric too long. Washing your shirts as soon as possible after wearing can prevent perspiration stains from setting in and will lengthen the life of your shirts.

Addressing the Laundry Problem

Many men's retailers have been experiencing problems with laundry abuse of their customers' shirts.

You should be aware of some of the problems and errors in laundering, and understand how to care for a good cotton shirt.

Avoid Heat and Bleach

Cotton fabric tends to "give up" dirt, so warm (not hot) water and soap or mild detergent are enough to get a cotton shirt clean. Excessive heat in the washer or dryer will shorten the life of your shirt.

Chlorine bleach should never be used, not even on white shirts. Bleach can turn the brightest white to yellow, and deep burgundies to pink. All sulphur-based dyes will turn pink when bleached. If garments are bleached and not rinsed properly, the chloride buildup in the fabrics can deteriorate them. Chlorine bleach can cut the life of a shirt in half.

Some Poor Laundry Practices

Some of the washing practices that are harmful include the improper use of chemicals, particularly the souring process, which occurs during the rinsing cycle. Souring is the treatment of garments in dilute acid, and its purpose is the neutralization of any alkali that is present.

The International Fabricare Institute states that "sour cannot be eliminated from commercial laundering (due to yellowing and sticking during pressing)." However, The International Fabricare Institute's test results, published in their "All About Shirts" pamphlet (published in 1992, but now out of print), show "oversouring, with any type of sour, would result in rapid degradation of colored yarns."

If souring is done improperly, it can harm the fabric. Many fine shirtings use reactive dyes because the shade range and available styling is so extensive. Some fibers that have been dyed using reactive dyes will react with sours and disintegrate in the laundry process. Improper souring can eat the stripes right out of your shirt.

The International Fabricare Institute further states that "the results of work done by a dye manufacturer concluded that the degradation is a result of an ion exchange which takes place when the fiber reactive dyed yarn is heated in an acidic state. To prevent degradation, the pH of the fabric must not be below 6.5." (pH is the value indicating the acidity or alkalinity of a material. A pH of 7.0 is neutral; less than 7.0 is acidic.)

"Testing at IFI indicates that yarn degradation did not occur when shirts were laundered in a formula where the pH of the sour was controlled to no lower than 6.5."

In the May, 1992 Bulletin, the IFI told its members: "In an attempt to satisfy consumers, the laundry industry must modify its procedures. This modification should be made swiftly because it is feasible and economically viable."

There are now "pH-controlled" or "buffered" sours on the market. Request that your launderer use them to ensure that your shirts will last longer. As noted earlier, bleach is not only unnecessary, it is actually destructive to cottons, including whites.

Just as a heavy oxford shirt can withstand a day of mountain-climbing better than a fine Sea Island cotton, different fabrics should be treated differently when laundering.

Understanding the Problem

All fabrics are made from yarns and all yarns are made from fibers. Fibers are spun into white or off-white yarn. When a fabric is a solid color it usually has been dyed in the fabric, or woven, state. For striped fabrics, the yarn is usually dyed before it is woven. The depth of dye penetration of the yarns is very important. When the yarns are woven into a fabric and exposed to wear and laundering procedures, they will begin to deteriorate or break down. If the fabric is bleached, or the color-fastness is disturbed in some other way, the tolerance of those fibers is destroyed. That's why in time, as the fabric continues to deteriorate from this early abuse, you may see the colored areas appear to fade or be eaten away, while some other parts of the garment remain intact.

Once a garment is abused with bleach or other chemicals, it continues to deteriorate. The weakening of the yarns may be invisible at first, but, even if the shirt is properly laundered from then on, the deterioration will continue. Fabric suppliers, such as Ezrasons Inc. and Threadtex Inc., confirm that it is impossible to tell, after the garment has been abused, whether the most recent laundry process is the culprit. The destruction could have begun long before.

Choosing a Laundry

If you're not inclined to wash your own shirts, it is important to find a good, reputable laundry that knows how to care for them properly.

Try to find a laundry that does the washing and pressing right on the premises. Ask questions. Find out how your shirts are being laundered. You want a laundry that does not use extremely large loads or extremely high temperatures. Make sure that they are aware that chlorine bleach and improper souring can harm your garment. Ask if they are using a "pH-controlled" or "buffered" sour.

Remember, your laundry has the responsibility to follow the instructions on the care tag in your garment.

Wear Life Expectancy

In their "All About Shirts" pamphlet, published in 1992), The International Fabricare Institute of The Association of Professional Dry Cleaners and Launderers reports that "The Fair Claims Guide, the industry guideline, states that shirts have a two-year wear life expectancy. The number of launderings is a better measuring method. The average shirt should have a wear life of 35 to 50 washings. This will fluctuate depending on the amount of abrasion and strain placed on the shirt during wear, the fiber content, the type of fabric, and the laundering procedure."

A shirt that is worn once a week should last approximately one year. If you have at least 12 shirts, including duplicates of your favorites, you can rotate them. This rotation is important in extending the life of your shirts.

If you must use a laundry, as most of us do, pay the extra money to have your shirts hand-done on hangers. This slight additional expense will extend the life of your shirts and pay for itself many times over. Also, remember that the less starch used, the longer the shirt will last. The heat the laundry uses when applying starch is the enemy — not the starch.

The Home Option

The safest way to maintain your shirts is to launder them at home, where you have total control.

Machine wash warm, do not use chlorine bleach, tumble dry medium, warm iron. Wash dark colors separately.

If you choose to press your own shirts, here are a few pointers:

- Make sure your iron is not too hot or it will scorch your shirt.
- Cotton should be ironed damp, so sprinkle the shirts prior to pressing, or use a can of spray starch or "Magic Sizing". Spray each small area before ironing.
- Iron the sleeves and cuffs first, then the shoulders, followed by the yoke. Next, do the front and back, leaving the collar for last. The collar should always be ironed away from the point.
- Go back and touch up any spots that you missed.

The Compromise

Many people are unwilling or unable to iron their shirts properly.

Consider washing your shirts at home, avoiding all harsh chemicals, bleach and excessive heat; then simply take them to the laundry to be pressed. Make a wash load of only your shirts and put them through an extra rinse to remove any harmful residue of detergents.

Given the time and craftsmanship that is involved in the making of a fine shirt, we should do all we can to protect and prolong the life of the garment.

Cotton is a strong fabric and, with the proper care, should provide you with long-lasting, comfortable shirts.

Common Laundry Questions:

Here are some of the more commonly-asked questions at The Shirt Store:

Q: *Should I remove the plastic collar stays before laundering my shirts?*

A: Yes. Washing the stays causes no harm, but pressing causes an outline of the stays to show on your collar and this may take several launderings to disappear.

Q: *What is the correct way to iron a monogram on a shirt?*

A: Place your iron on the monogram and iron away from it to avoid bunching the fabric around the stitching. This is the same principle you use when you avoid pleating on a collar by ironing away from the points.

Q: *How can an ink stain be removed from a shirt?*

A: Spray the ink stain with hair spray (the stickier the better), or soak for a few hours in milk, and then launder as usual.

Q: *How can marks from a pencil be removed from a shirt?*

A: Use an eraser, then wash.

Q: *What can I do if I forget my collar stays?*

A: Cut substitutes from any thin, rigid material that is available, such as cardboard or a seldom-used credit card. Paper clips bent to the correct length also work.

Q: *How can I get the wrinkles out of a shirt without an iron?*

A: Hang the shirt in the bathroom while you shower, and leave it in the room to dry overnight.

Q: *How can I get a perspiration stain out of my shirt?*

A: Before laundering, soak the shirt for 24 hours in salty water.

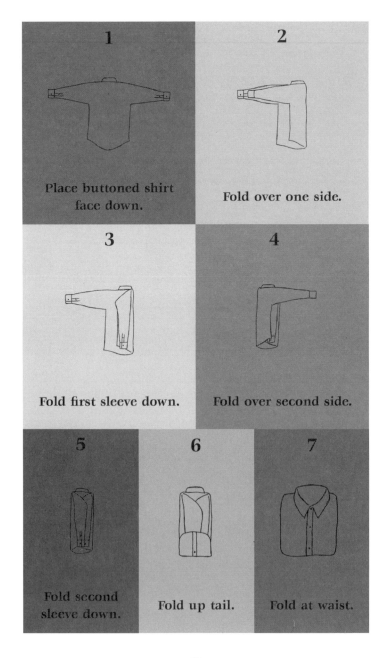

1. Place buttoned shirt face down.
2. Fold over one side.
3. Fold first sleeve down.
4. Fold over second side.
5. Fold second sleeve down.
6. Fold up tail.
7. Fold at waist.

Shirt Construction

Manufacturing in the U.S.A.

Over the years, many manufacturers have moved their manufacturing overseas, primarily in an effort to reduce costs. Despite some of the apparent cost advantages this can provide, we are convinced that, when everything is considered, manufacturing in the U.S.A. is the right thing for The Shirt Store.

For years, I have subcontracted cutting and sewing to the Barnesboro Shirt Company in Barnesboro, PA. The factory, which is 300 miles west of New York City, is close enough to allow me to regularly inspect the quality of the work being done at the factory. And, believe me, manufacturing one of our shirts is a complex process — 52 sewing operations, including 13 or 14 for collars alone. And that's for our stock shirts, not custom-made!

Even more important, having the plant this close makes it possible for The Shirt Store to be a fashion setter instead of a follower. When I have an idea for a new shirt, I can work closely with the factory and see the results in weeks, not months, as is usually the case with plants overseas. By working directly with Yale Shanfield, who owns the plant, I can adjust my product line to quickly respond to new fashion trends and immediate customer needs.

SHIRT CONSTRUCTION

How Do You Know If Your Shirt's Well-made?

You should get the best shirt for your money. Here are some features to look for in a well-constructed shirt:

Single-needle Stitching

The seams are stitched down one side, then down the other side, each time with one needle to form a lockstitch. This is the finest and strongest formation that can be used. Double-needle stitching, which sews both sides of the seam at the same time, using a double needle, is cheaper and faster for the manufacturer, but can cause the seams to pucker when laundered.

Tight, Close Stitches

The tighter the stitch (the more stitches per inch), the stronger your shirt will be. The stitches should be difficult to count, but if your eyes are good, you should see at least 18 stitches per inch. If there are fewer, the seams will open more easily.

Vertical Seam on the Yoke

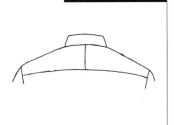

Custom shirtmakers use a split yoke so they can adjust the height of each shoulder separately. A good ready-made shirt will be styled with a vertical seam on the yoke to follow this tradition. This feature is called a "split" yoke.

Vertical Seam on the Yoke

Placket Button

This button that closes the gap on the sleeve used to be called a gauntlet button. It was originally used so the cuffs could be rolled back when washing. This handy button now closes the gap at the wrist and is considered a sign of a well-styled garment.

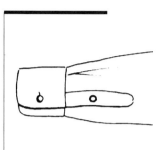

The Placket Button

Pleats at Cuff

Look for a couple of pleats where the sleeve meets the cuff. This is an extra touch that is more difficult to achieve, but adds style to the shirt, and also a better fit in the arm area.

Exact Sleeve Lengths

Buy only shirts that are sized to your exact length. They will fit you better. Avoid the average sleeve length shirts that are sized 32/33, 34/35, etc.

Buttons

Buttons should be well secured so that they stay on during laundering.

A Front Placket/Center Pleat

A plain closing is not as strong as one with a stitched-down fold of fabric down the front, called a placket or center pleat.

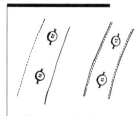

Plain versus Placket Front

Linings

Cotton shirts should use 100% cotton linings so that the shrinkage factor is the same in both lining and fabric. Resin is added to the lining to hold the finish and keep the shape.

The choice of a soft lining on the button-down, and the heavier lining on the non-button-down collars will help insure a proper look. I use a fusible lining in the collars of my non-button-down stock shirts to help eliminate the laundry problem of creasing collars. The lining is fused to the top of the collar leaf, using an adhesive resin applied with heat and pressure. This process makes it much easier to iron the collar smoothly after laundering.

The choice of the correct width and weight of top-center lining is important to make the shirt hold up through many launderings.

The weight of the French cuff lining and the button-cuff lining can be the difference between a crisp finish and a limp cuff.

Fabric

Finally, or perhaps first of all, choose a shirt made of 100% cotton.

Polyester blends will not hold up as well and will never be as crisp looking after laundering as 100% cotton.

The Shirt Size Mystery

The man who shops for himself has discovered that the simple shirt size has become a mystery. Years ago, he could go into a store and ask for a shirt by knowing his neck and sleeve size. No longer. He now has to ask several questions:

Is the shirt a full-cut shirt? Are the sleeve lengths exact? Is the collar size cut for shrinkage? Is the sleeve length cut for shrinkage? How long are the tails?

Once it is determined that the answers are satisfactory, he has to be concerned with label. Labels become important because the sizing on private labels in a department store will change depending on where the shirt is manufactured. If the store purchases stock from different manufacturers, the label may remain the same and the sizing can change.

The best way to make sure of getting the right size is to measure your neck and sleeve and then ask if the shirt is cut true to size. Then, try on the shirt.

In a cotton shirt, there should be $1/2$" excess room in the collar and $1/2$" to $3/4$" in the sleeve to allow for residual shrinkage. If the shirt fits perfectly before it is laundered, it's too small; if there's more than the allowances given, it's too big.

Fit

Comfort should be the determining factor in fit.

The neckband of the **collar** should never choke. If it is too tight, it will spread or curl the collar, increase the tie space where the knot sits, or pull the points up from the chest. The band should be snug enough to keep the collar from falling away from the neck and down the chest. Remember, you can get away with a shirt collar that is a little loose far better than you can a tight collar.

The **body** of the shirt should be full for your personal comfort. The taper should never bind the chest or midriff.

Four inches above body measurement is considered a tapered shirt. Only the man who does not have a bulging middle should consider this option.

Today's look has softer lines than the look of the 80's. The trend in fashion is toward a looser fit in dress clothes as well as sportswear. A good guideline is eight inches above body measurement. If your shirt has more, it tends to look unkempt and tapering is in order.

Fuller garments can be eight to ten inches above measurements. The heavier man should wear his shirt larger so that he won't have any gaps, especially when he sits down.

Fine stores will offer a tapering service to tailor their stock shirts to your torso.

The **tail** of the shirt should be at least five inches below the waist to stay in the trousers, but not so long that it has to be bunched up. The average tail length in a standard dress shirt is about 31 inches and extra long tails would be about 34 inches.

The **sleeves** should be long enough to allow you to bend your arm without pulling the cuff away from your wrist.

Be sure you like the feel as well as the look of your shirt when judging the fit.

Measuring.
Here's how to do it:

Neck — Some manufacturers put size tabs in their shirts that inadvertently mislead the man on his collar size. If you want to know your true collar size, there are two easy ways with a tape measure:

You can have a friend measure you, starting at the base of the neck under your Adam's Apple and bringing the tape around your neck to meet at the start. Place it where the collar will sit; higher on the neck will make the collar very uncomfortable, as it will pull when buttoned. When there is enough slack to make you comfortable, that is the collar size you should wear.

Or, if you have a shirt that you are very comfortable in, measure the collar from the center of the button to the edge of the buttonhole while holding the collar taut.

Remember, some people like more room in the collar and others like it snug. The ideal is to be comfortable while still looking good. Generally, the collar should fit closely enough so you can just slide your little finger into the space between collar and neck.

However, comfort is the key — some men prefer looser collars. A collar that is slightly loose prevents a muscular neck from appearing too thick. Also, if a man is putting on weight it can make him appear that he is losing weight.

If the collar fits you well unlaundered, then it is too tight.

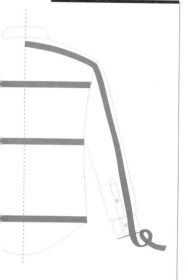

Cotton shirts will shrink at least $\frac{1}{2}$" in the laundering process in the first few launderings.

Sleeve — Have a friend put the end of the tape measure at the center of your back and the base of your neck, then pull it across the shoulder and down your arm, making sure that they've gone over any muscle of your shoulder and arm. Have them measure to the break of the wrist and add one inch. This will allow room for the bending of the arm, and will allow you to show cuff if your jacket is tailored properly.

If you want to measure the sleeve length yourself, use a shirt you are comfortable in. Lay it on a flat surface and measure the sleeve, starting at the center of the back at the collar, go across the shoulder and down to the end of the sleeve.

Custom Shirts

I think we should address the option of having your shirts custom made, and define exactly what custom means.

Custom shirts, or bespoke, as the English say, are shirts made from an individual pattern for the specific customer according to his specific measurements and style requirements. This is very different from made-to-measure, which is accomplished by simply altering a stock pattern or stock pattern pieces to a customer's measurements. In this method, the result can be very inconsistent.

Each time you order true custom shirts, your own paper pattern is used to cut the cloth. Consequently, each time you order, the results will be the same. "You can only acquire fit with true custom using a paper pattern," says our pattern/shirtmaker George Bijimenian.

When you order made-to-measure, you will have someone translate your measurements and alter the stock pattern. Since there is no individual pattern on file for you, there is no way to ensure that the alterations to the pattern will come out the same each time. You can get different results depending on who does the translating and measuring.

Made-to-measure almost always works well for the customer who is a standard size and does not require unusual styling. The customer who has a fit problem or very different styling requirements will do much better with custom.

Since not all shirtmakers define their terms the same,

make sure you know what you're getting when you order "custom" shirts. Ask the tailor if he makes a full paper pattern from scratch, and be sure the final sample is exactly what you want before you approve it.

The Process of "Custom"

The process of custom begins with precise measuring — not only collar size and sleeve length, but yoke, chest, half-chest, waist, hip, biceps, forearms, wrists, and length of shirttail — and allowances have to be made for characteristics that are hard to quantify, such as concave chest areas, slope of the shoulder areas, roundness of the back, etc.

When the client tries on his first sample, there may be adjustments. The pattern will be adjusted, so all shirts made from it will be identical, giving the client the fit he wants.

Styling Options

Proper fit is undoubtedly important, but it is the design factor that excites many customers. In my experience, about 70% do custom for fit and 90% do it for styling. Even the customer with fit problems enjoys the options of styling and fabric selection available when doing custom. They soon get caught up in the fun and excitement of designing their own shirts and having it done their own way. The selections of fabric are vast and the options on styling limitless. Because the pattern is made from scratch, anything, within reason, that the customer wants can be done.

What you wear reflects your personality, and in custom shirts that is especially true, since the choice is truly yours.

Color and Pattern in Business Shirts

Since it's no longer necessary to play by the old rule of "solid shirt with striped or patterned suit", and patterns are mixed very freely, you are no longer forced to look like everyone else even though you, too, have a navy pinstripe suit. The navy pinstripe suit can take a conservative approach with a classic straight-collar shirt in white, or become dashing with a spread-collar blue stripe with contrasting white collar and white French cuffs.

A different collar style, or color, or pattern, can give the suit a new look. By rotating your shirts and ties with your suits, you can present a slightly different image at different times. It will change the look of that suit and make the old one look new.

When you choose your wardrobe, picking the patterns of your shirts can be your expression of individual taste and personality. The dress shirt is no longer just a utilitarian garment. It's becoming a fashion statement on its own.

The style or color of one's shirt can reflect a mood or make a statement. Having a number of different styles and colors in the closet allows the well-groomed individual to be able to achieve the right look for any occasion.

- If you are feeling poorly and want to give your look a lift, try wearing a bold striped shirt in two colors on a white background with French cuffs, instead of that solid blue pinpoint with button cuffs.

- If you have a meeting where you are not sure of the tastes of the others attending, pull out the perfectly pressed white shirt. If you need to go out to dinner, make sure you wear one with French cuffs.
- If you are being filmed for a TV spot for your company, the blue end-on-end would be a perfect choice.
- If you have to leave the office and drive to the country, the button-down oxford would be the winner.

In business, you must remember to dress the part. Your choice of clothing determines which group you will be identified with. Make sure your shirt reflects your choice.

Dress-Down Days

In September 1994 we did a study on the "dress-down" trend. We found that the dress-shirt market is changing and the changes are, if nothing else, colorful.

Art Cooper is editor-in-chief of *GQ*, where fashion is the name of the game, yet he tells us that his magazine has a very informal policy with no dress restrictions whatsoever.

"Magazines, ad agencies, and other creative environments are a lot looser, when it comes to dress, than Wall Street, banking, real estate, and even the business side of publishing," says Cooper. "Salespeople must dress the part to inspire confidence and so on, but inside, where people are sitting at their PC's writing and editing all day, it's important to be comfortable.

"I absolutely believe that people do better work when they are comfortable," responded Cooper to our inquiry. But the fashion-conscious people at *GQ* are still very stylish, even when they are comfortably dressed.

This, however, is by no means the end of traditional business wear. There are still as many companies who frown on the dress-down looks as there are who promote them. Before making any decisions, check out the decision makers in your company and follow their lead.

WARDROBE OPTIONS
Solids

You should concentrate on building a wardrobe of solid shirts first (even if the solids are only white and blue) before concentrating on your patterned options. We've chosen nine solids in our Basic Dozen (page 76).

The rule used to be that when solid colors (other than white) were worn, you had to go light. The lightest colors you could find — ivory, ecru, pale blue, pale pink, light yellow, soft gray.

Because of the new freedom of the 90's this is no longer always true. Depending on your position and the occasion the dark-colored solids can be very appropriate.

The colors that were only seen in patterns, such as navy, wine red, dark grey and even black can be seen in many offices during the day. The increased popularity of black can be attributed to the entertainment industry. Arsenio Hall and other TV stars sparked the interest in black, olive and greens.

My advice, however, is to buy your basics first. Add spice to the wardrobe later with the darks.

Stick to the white, medium blues, ecrus, and light grays first — they are the neutrals. You don't have to worry when matching your suit and tie. Next, add the pink, yellow and helio. Be sure of yourself and the setting before wearing the dark shirt. There are still many people who dislike them and not everyone looks good in them.

Patterns

Patterns have always offered more leeway in colors for business shirts. Any pale color you would use for a solid shirt looks good in a patterned one. In addition, the dark colors are not only appropriate but very handsome for patterned business shirts. My favorites are on a white or very pale ground, or a pattern-on-pattern look such as the Glen Plaids, which simply look like interesting solids.

Save the dark plaids for the weekend.

Remember, however, pattern of any kind is considered less formal than a solid color.

Let's look at the most popular.

Checks

Remember, checks (a pattern of squares) are always considered more casual than stripes. Here are some favorites.

Glen Plaid is a small, even check pattern. It is usually done in color-on-color, giving it the basic appearance of a solid shirt, especially from a distance.

Mini-check is a small check, usually one color on white. It is more casual than stripes, but more dressy than larger checks or tattersalls. This is the one we've chosen for our Basic Dozen.

Tattersall Check is a traditional check pattern of two sets of dark lines in a regularly spaced check design on a light ground. The classic coloring is red and black on cream, although many other colorings are found today. Blankets in this pattern were used on horses in the London market founded by Richard Tattersall in 1766. It soon became a popular material for vests for sportswear and is now popular for shirting fabrics. The most popular colors today are red-and-black or blue-and-black on white.

Windowpane Check is a plain, barred plaid similar to the pattern of panes in a window. Its bigger pattern gives it a more casual look than the mini-checks or tattersalls. This larger pattern does have one drawback — it is harder to coordinate with ties and suits.

Stripes

Stripes are an important part of the business shirt wardrobe. We've chosen three for our Basic Dozen. Here are some of the more popular.

Hairline Stripes are narrow stripes, about the width of a hair. The effect is that of a solid, and can be worn without regard to its pattern when coordinating with suits and ties. Because of this flexibility it is part of our Basic Dozen.

Pinstripe is a very fine stripe, less than $\frac{1}{16}$". Its name comes from the fact that the stripes are the width of a straight pin. You can't go wrong with this stripe. It is a pattern that looks good with most suits and ties. It is also included in our Basic Dozen.

Pencil Stripes are a little wider than pinstripes—about $1/16$". It is at this width that the fabric can be said to be a definite stripe, not just a patterned solid.

Wider Stripes are any stripes over $1/16$" wide. Because every basic wardrobe should have a bolder option, the wider stripe is part of our Basic Dozen. Keep in mind that the wider the stripe and the darker the color, the bolder it becomes. For this reason, stripes $1/2$" and wider tend to be used primarily in casual shirts.

Multi-Colored Stripes are usually seen in more expensive shirtings. It is wise to stick to no more than two colors plus white for shirts you wear for business. When there are more than three colors in a shirt, it is more appropriate for casual wear.

Other Patterns

Solid colored weaves are achieved by changing the arrangement of the weaving threads.

"White-on-Whites" is the term used for all-white shirts with patterned weaves.

Herringbone is a zigzag woven pattern suggesting the skeleton of a fish. This can be worn just like a solid shirt. This is a good example of the difference texture can make.

Colors

White is Always Right

White was reported to be the #1 best-selling color in dress shirts last spring, and is predicted to be #1 again this fall.

We did a customer survey to determine buying preferences and found that in spite of the ebb and flow of fashion trends, white shirts remain most favored by men.

Asked why they favor white shirts, more than two thirds of the respondents said that in addition to being "correct attire for every occasion," wearing a white shirt can never be viewed as "upstaging" one's clients who may not be fashion conscious. Because white is always right; it is always appropriate.

"The white shirt," said one customer, "is totally non-threatening and makes no statement about the wearer other than that he is neat and businesslike." One respondent stated that a white shirt subliminally conveys "virtue" — quite a feat for the simple shirt!

"When it comes to new business meetings or client meetings," said the CEO of a major PR agency, "it's better to be safe and non-controversial."

Another factor noted by my customers was that, if one is traveling and cannot change for the evening, a white shirt will carry its wearer through the day, especially if one is wearing French cuffs which bring a "dressed-up" look to cocktails or dinner meetings. Presented in the right style, it is considered dressy enough for the most formal occasions.

"Moreover," said one of our Shirt Store customers, "if you want to keep the chore of packing down to a minimum, white shirts go with everything."

For that classic look, a basic white shirt and standard collar will never let you down.

A white shirt is the perfect interview shirt. It will allow you to be judged for your own personal qualities not your choice of pattern or color. On the interview, you should never chance having your shirt make the statement instead of you. The white shirt is the easy answer.

White is the only color that goes with every suit and every tie in a man's wardrobe.

Almost 50% of the shirts we sell each year are white and that's why they make up 50% of our Basic Dozen (page 76).

In short, white is always right!

Choosing the Right White Fabric

Remember, when choosing white, fabric choice is very important. Each fabric will look and feel different.

Broadcloths and oxfords are the two fabrics that we see most in the white business shirt. You can tell the difference between the two if you remember that the broadcloths are smoother and more translucent and the oxfords are softer, heavier and less translucent.

Let's take a look at the most popular choices.

Broadcloth, whether single-ply or two-ply, is a fine smooth cotton. It will have a sheen to the cloth and be perceived as a very dressy shirt. It looks best with the dressy suit and tie.

Broadcloth can come in many different qualities of fabric. The tighter the weave, the silkier the cloth.

In the single-ply fabrics, pima will have the longest staple and, therefore, the nicest "hand".

The 100's two-ply will have the most body of the two-plies. Because of this, it will wrinkle the least. If you like starch, this is the broadcloth to choose. In The Shirt Store, we refer to this fabric as "Egyptian."

Fabrics that are 120's two-ply or more are usually done in broadcloths, and often referred to as "Sea Island." They are the silkiest of weaves and the most luxurious on your body.

Remember that even the tightest woven of the broad-cloths — the Sea Island qualities — will be translucent. If you are concerned about this aspect, broadcloth, no matter how expensive, should not be your choice.

Oxford is a cotton shirting fabric with a small basketweave surface. It has a full texture. It is soft and comfortable. It is lustrous than broadcloth and considered less formal

Single-Ply oxford is usually done in button-down styles, because it has a more casual look than the two ply oxfords. This heavy, beefy cotton is able to take more abuse than the lighter, finer weaves.

Pinpoint is two-ply oxford. It is dressier than single-ply and usually is done in 80's two-ply. This oxford can dress-up the button-down, and when made into a tab collar with French cuff can take it out to a "night on the town." French oxford is another two-ply oxford — this one with a weave. It is silky and lustrous.

Remember that all types of oxfords will wear at the friction points — collars and cuffs more than broadcloths.

Voile is a fine, plain, almost transparent cotton cloth.

It is popular in the hot summer months because of its light-weight attributes. It, however, is always perceived as dressy and, in my opinion only right for evening wear.

White-on-White is usually done in a broadcloth. It is a white pattern on white. It is always perceived as dressy and again, in my opinion, only right for evening wear.

Blue is Number Two

Blue is a neutral, and as such can be worn with most suits and complements most ties. It is as comfortable with the new green and brown earth tone suits as it is with the tried and true blues and grays.

It is the perfect TV shirt, and is seen on more anchormen because it flatters most complexions. If your picture is being taken, and white is not required, blue should be your color choice.

Because blue is still conservative, it has been chosen by many as the safe option other than white.

Blue shirts come in many fabrics and patterns. Let's look at some of the options available.

The Blue Solid Shirt

All of the qualities talked about in white shirts will apply to blue solids. Some aspects of the cloth are different because of the color. Let's examine these differences.

Broadcloth — Whether it be single or two-ply, broadcloth is a fine smooth cotton with a marvelous sheen to the cloth that makes it a very dressy shirt. It looks best with the dressy suit and tie.

It has lost much of its popularity because it is restricted to the formal look, while some of the other choices can be dressed up or down.

Chambray is a cotton shirting fabric with a frosted effect produced by weaving white threads lengthwise, blue ones crosswise. Once only seen on informal shirts, it is now a staple in the business wardrobe. It is often styled with French cuffs and in the deep rich tones looks great with contrasting collars and cuffs. A deep blue chambray is a powerful choice for the green-hued suits of the 90's.

End-on-End is a madras cotton with a frosted or muted effect produced by weaving together white "end" (or lengthwise) threads with blue-colored crosswise threads; the result is similar to chambray. It can be dressed up or down easily and is a very light airy comfortable fabric. Its white overtones complement white collar and cuff styles. Because it is yarn dyed, it holds its color beautifully. Since the purpose of any good shirt collection is to give you options, this blue shirt is a part of our Basic Dozen.

Single-Ply Oxford in blue is more casual than white. The cross-weaves of white and blue are predominant and because of the texture, is limited to the casual suit or sportcoat.

Pinpoint is dressier than single-ply because the weave is tighter — the cross-weave of white simply gives the cloth a luster and sheen that can be dressed up as well as down. depending on the collar and cuff style chosen. While the button-down still keeps it casual, a white collar and cuff can be a very elegant look.

Two of these blue shirts are included in the Basic Dozen..

French oxford has a two-ply weave which makes the color become more lustrous. This option really dresses up the oxford. For this reason, I like styling it with French cuffs.

The Blue Patterned Shirt

The most important color in patterned shirts is blue. No other color is as neutral with the business suit and tie.

It is for this reason why we have chosen blue as the color for three of the four patterned shirts of our Basic Dozen — a hairline, a narrow stripe and a mini-check.

Burgundy follows

We believe white and blues make up 80 – 90% of the business dress shirt wardrobe.

The other leading color is burgundy, done in a stripe or check on a white ground. This is another neutral. I can't think of a suit color that it could not go with. Navys, grays, blacks, tans, browns and even greens are no trouble for this shirt. One thing to be careful of when wearing the burgundy shirt — do not wear a red tie. Even though you might think they are from the same color family, the brightness of the red is usually too much for the burgundy.

We have selected a burgundy stripe for our Basic Dozen.

THE OTHER COLORS

There are many other options for your business wardrobe, but until you have satisfied your basics they should not be considered.

When you have your basics, however, if you like a color — wear it. Enjoy your choices. Just make sure the color complements you, your suit and tie or your sport jacket.

Ecru

The ecru solid should be worn like a white shirt — it will go with everything and just soften the look.

Pink

Pink has experienced a resurgence in the business wardrobe. Men are no longer afraid of the color being too feminine. It is a color that can change the look of the blue or gray suit. It also looks good with the right shade of tan, brown, green or gray. It looks best with burgundy or helio accented ties.

Yellow

Yellow is easy to wear if it is a soft yellow. The brighter yellows look better when used in the pattern of the shirt. A yellow and blue stripe can be a wonderful addition to wear with the blue or gray suit. Yellow has always been a natural with the brown and green hues.

Helio

Helio, or lavender, is worn like pink. Most suits that would go with your pink shirts would be complemented by the helio shirt. This color still frightens many men and is considered a high fashion item.

Red

Red should definitely only be worn in a patterned shirt. Only the very narrow stripes on white would be considered a dressy shirt. The color usually means casual. Red looks best with the blue or gray suit.

Gray

Gray in a light solid shade is a neutral. It can be worn with most suits. As the gray gets darker, it gets to look more casual and it becomes harder to match with a suit. The gray stripe can be worn more easily than a black stripe. Because it is lighter in tone it will blend in easier with your suit. The gray striped shirt is a great option for the gray toned suit. The tie can be the brightest red or blue and still look great.

Green

Green solid, unless it is very pale, is not considered a dress shirt option. The green stripe, however, if it is not too wide can be a great change for the navy, gray, tan, brown or even green suit. Green comes in so many shades, before adding it to your collection, make sure the tone is complementary to your suits.

Black

Black has always been accepted if it is used in a narrow stripe. It is dramatic with the gray or black suit. It can complement the tan or green with the right tie that "ties it all together." In a solid, it is definitely perceived as a dress-down look.

Brown

Brown should also be pattern-on-white to keep it in the business wardrobe. The suits that the brown shirt is best with are, of course, browns, tans or greens. Solid brown is too casual, except for the dress-down look.

Details on Business Shirts

An easy rule — the fewer details the better.

The Two Acceptable Details: Pockets and Monograms
Pockets

If you have use for a pocket, you should have one. It is an acceptable feature of a business dress shirt, and is the preference of 90% of our customers.

Monograms

A monogram, tastefully done and placed, can be the final touch of elegance that transforms a shirt from a quality garment to a personal expression that makes that shirt uniquely yours. The monogram's popularity has increased and is now accepted in even the most conservative environments.

Whether or not to monogram your shirt is a very personal decision.

We asked Ethel Stern, owner of Monogram It! in New York, what the monogram says about the person wearing the shirt. "The monogram's ultimate message is, 'I am an important person,'" says Mrs. Stern. She points out, however, that "the message should be followed by the words, 'in my humble opinion,' so the monogram must be understated."

A monogram that is too bold, or too large, or appears in more than one place on the shirt counteracts this idea and loses its class and distinction and becomes garish and gaudy. Rule to remember, use initials — not complete names and stay no more than $1/4$" high. and you will be safe.

Many men choose to monogram because a monogram has always been perceived as belonging on custom or more expensive shirts. They feel that with monograms, their shirts will be perceived as more expensive. Not only is this debatable, but this is not a reason to monogram a shirt.

Prince Philip, the Duke of Edinburgh, does not wear monogrammed shirts, while Prince Charles does. John Kennedy always had a small JFK embroidered on his pocket or sleeve.

The point is that there are just as many men who like monograms as who don't. So, only monogram if you like it!

Placement

Historically, the pocket has been the most popular place for a monogram — top center or middle of the pocket are the two most common choices. With the growing popularity of the French cuff, the left cuff has become a common choice for the cuff link wearer, especially in the United States. Shirts without pockets are typically monogrammed where the pocket would be, or lower on the left panel (about five to six inches up from the waist) — the "European" placement. Other placements we have seen are on the sleeve, just above the elbow (popular with our Japanese clients) and the tail of the shirt (used mostly for laundry identification).

Color

Good taste should be the final arbiter in choosing the color for your monogram.

The monogram color may match or be contrasted with the color of the shirt. The more conservative approach is to match the color, e.g., using a navy monogram on a blue shirt, burgundy on a burgundy stripe, etc. Two colors that are neutral and appropriate for all suits and ties are gray and navy. You may want to use the same color and style on all your shirts, regardless of their color, as a sort of trademark that never varies.

White-on-white is very understated and is sometimes used just for laundry identification purposes. As a matter of fact, when the practice of monogramming began in the seventeenth century, the purpose was to put the family mark on valuable linens. The type of jacket worn in those days did not even allow the shirt to show. It was not until the twentieth century, when jackets started coming off, that the monogram was seen.

Types

Once you have chosen a style, color, and placement for your monogram, you must decide on hand-made versus machine-made monograms. The handmade monograms are raised more than the machine-made versions, and they can usually be made smaller, if desired. Of course, as with any handmade item, the cost is greater.

If you choose a monogram style in which the middle initial is larger than the other two, it is customary to put the initial letter of your surname in the center. When all three letters are the same size, your first, middle and last initials will be in order.

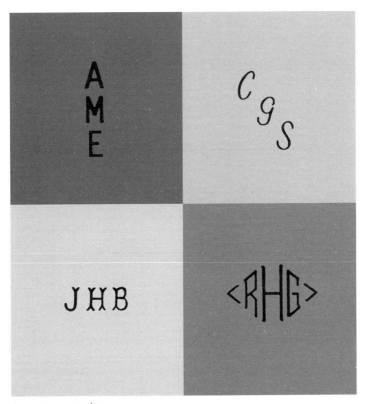

Some monogram styles

Formalwear

Informal Formalwear?

Times have changed and even the most formal occasions have become more casual. The banded collar tuxedo shirt is now seen even at the most conservative affairs. Black-tie optional affairs now can have as many dark suits as tuxedos. We are, without a doubt, becoming a less formal society.

Weddings, especially, have seen the traditional formal attire replaced by less formal suits and non-white shirts. Even if they wear the traditional white they are opting for non-traditional collar styles such as the "club" or "tab" to achieve a distinctive look.

However, if you are working in a business environment, and have attendant social obligations, the chances are you will adhere to the traditional formalwear of the past. It is for these occasions, and for those who appreciate elegance, that I have included this section in our book.

Traditional Formalwear

My friend, Marshall Dutko, owner of Baldwin Formal in New York, reminds us that "formalwear, as we now call it, was the everyday dress for the gentlemen of society. Cutaway coats were worn during the daytime, while white tie and tailcoats were worn after six o'clock in the evening.

"In the late 1800's, an upstart named Lorillard changed

formal fashion forever. He had his tailor remove the tail from his full-dress coat and modify its length. He wore this outfit, with a black tie, to an evening function in Tuxedo Park, New York. The 'tuxedo' was born."

A tuxedo or dinner jacket can transform any man into a Cary Grant or Fred Astaire. As he fastens his bow tie he becomes instantly debonair.

Whether you own your own tuxedo or rent one, a properly fitted shirt is indispensable for you to achieve that "look" that makes wearing formalwear an occasion.

Formal Shirts

Whether black-tie or white-tie, the formal tuxedo shirt is traditionally white, and has traditionally been French cuffed.

There are two types of collars that are acceptable — the wing or the lay-down classic collar.

The **wing** is the more formal of the two and is by its nature a high collar. The shorter-necked man might have trouble in the wing collar, while the long-necked man will look especially attractive. This collar is used with all types of tuxedo fronts.

The **classic (straight) collar** is the other acceptable collar. It is generally more comfortable than the wing. This is usually seen on pleated front shirts.

There are three basic front finishes for tuxedo shirts.

The most traditional is the **pleated front**. The pleats can vary in width from a $1/8$" woven pin-tuck to a 1" sewn pleat. The most common is the $1/4$" to $1/2$" pleat. These shirts should have a button-hole front to accommodate studs. Today, most manufacturers provide four stud holes and four studs in jewelry sets. If you have older jewelry, you might only have three studs — make sure your jewelry and shirt match.

Another style that has become popular again is the **fly front**. It uses buttons, but they are hidden under a strip of cloth. Many men prefer this because they don't have to fuss with studs.

The third front style, and my personal favorite, is the **pique front**. This shirt is made with a bib of pique on a French front (turned under with no center pleat). The collar and cuff are also made from matching pique. The wing collar is usually used to complete this most elegant look. It was meant to be worn on only the most formal occasions with the full-dress or tailcoat, but as formalwear has become less traditional, the pique is seen with every type of evening wear.

Helpful Formal Hints:

Q: *Do I wear the bow-tie behind or in front of my winged collar?*

A: It is traditional to wear the bow tie behind the wing tips, but it is also acceptable to wear the tie in front.

Q: *Is it proper to wear suspenders or a cummerbund with my tuxedo?*

A: Suspenders should always be worn with your tuxedo. The trousers do not come with belt loops and the cummerbund does not act like a belt, so, even when wearing a cummerbund, you must wear suspenders. The cummerbund should not be worn with a double-breasted tuxedo because it is too bulky under the jacket designed to be worn closed. Cummerbunds should always be worn with single-breasted tuxedos if you are not wearing a vest — it is a nice finishing touch.

Q: *Do I wear my pleats up or down on my cummerbund?*

A: The pleats should be worn facing up! In the past, little pockets were found in the pleats to hold a coin, the theater tickets, or a key. That is why the pleats always turn up.

How Many Shirts Do You Need?

The answer is, of course, as many as you can afford and as many as you can store.

Another measure is at least 4-5 shirts per suit.

Because cotton must be laundered after each use and because most of us send our shirts out to be done, you need to have enough to tide you over when the others are at the launderers.

My basic rule is that every man who regularly wears suits needs at least two dozen shirts in his closet. Of these, the first 12 should come from what I describe as the *Basic Dozen.*

These 12 (actually 13, because Shirt Store customers get the 13th shirt free with each dozen they buy) basic shirts can, of course, vary from person to person. But, if you compare the wardrobes of well-dressed men, the basic shirts in those wardrobes are remarkably similar. Here's my *Basic Dozen:*

THE BASIC DOZEN

Six white shirts, six blue shirts and one burgundy.

Nine with regular cuffs and four with French cuffs.

One shirt with white collar and white French cuffs.

Three collar styles: two button-downs, six classic collars,

and five modified-spreads.

Nine solid shirts and four with patterns.

Three striped shirts and one with checks.

THE WHITES

Fabric selection is up to you because comfort is such a personal decision. You may even choose to mix the fabrics, to give your collection more variety.

First we should include **one button-down**. We recommend a pinpoint oxford, because it can be dressed up or down more easily than any other fabric.

Second, we have **three classic straight collars**, **one with French cuffs and two with button cuffs**. We have chosen our button-cuffs in single-ply broadcloth and the French cuff in the more lustrous and dressy Egyptian 100's two-ply broadcloth.

Last, we have **two modified spreads**, **one with French cuffs** in Egyptian again, and a pinpoint oxford in **a button cuff**.

THE BLUES

We suggest the following fabrics and styles for these six.

First we have **one button-down**. We have chosen a **solid pinpoint oxford** again, because it can be dressed up or down as the occasion demands.

Second, we have chosen **one classic collared "end-on-end" with button cuffs** because it too can be worn with the business suit and tie, or dressed-down with a sport coat and tie, or even worn open with jeans.

Next, we have selected **two broadcloth stripes. One hairline stripe on white with classic collar and French cuffs, and one narrow stripe on white with a modified spread collar and button cuffs.** These two, although the same color, are so different in appearance that the suit will change with each use.

Our other pattern is a **mini-check in Egyptian broadcloth**. If you prefer a single-ply or glen plaid instead, that is fine. This shirt should be a **modified spread collar with French cuff** to add a distinctive touch to the wardrobe. Using the more casual pattern in a more dressy style says that you know what you're doing and are not afraid of change.

Our last selection to complete the blue assortment is the classic **white collar and cuff.** We have chosen a **Pinpoint oxford with a classic collar and French cuffs**.

THE BURGUNDY

For our last shirt, we have chosen a **burgundy pinstripe with a modified-spread collar and button cuff**. This selection will complement any suit in your wardrobe and will round out your "Bakers' Dozen".

The Shirt Accessories

In this section, we will briefly cover what we think of as the accessories to the shirt wardrobe — ties, suits, cufflinks, other jewelry, belts, socks, shoes, suspenders and pocket squares.

Let's start with the item that people will see as soon as they see your shirt — the tie.

TIES

The well-made tie.

The color and pattern of the tie are the first things that attract you, but you have to be sure that the tie is constructed so that it will knot well, drape properly and return to its original shape between wearings.

The components of a tie are the outer fabric (or shell), interlining, stitching, and tipping. A well-made tie combines quality outer fabric, "resilient construction" and properly constructed and coordinated interlining.

The only fabric we recommend for the shells of the ties in your business wardrobe is 100% silk. It is a natural fiber which drapes well, wears well, takes color beautifully when yarn-dyed or skein-dyed, and has a good "hand" or feel. A good silk tie can be worn at any time of the year. The variety of silks used for the shells are seemingly endless. There are woven silks (heavier than the light printed silks), twills,

Tie Construction

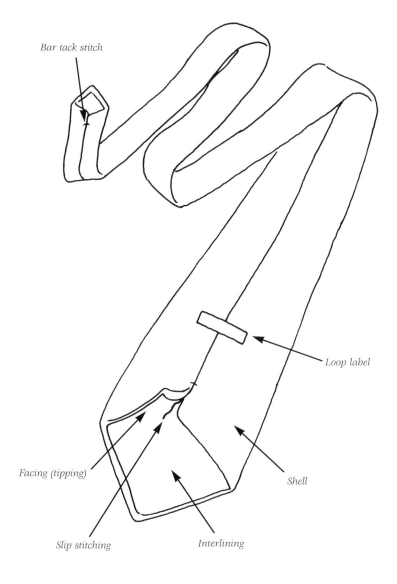

Bar tack stitch

Loop label

Facing (tipping)

Shell

Slip stitching

Interlining

crepe de chine, ancient madder and grenadine, to name but a few. They all have in common, however, that indefinable feel and luster that is the salient characteristic of silk.

The firmness is what will give body to the all-important knot, and that firmness is dependent on the lining of the tie. Choose a tie that is lined to the tip, so that it stays firm and keeps its shape.

The "hand" of the finished tie is also affected by the weight of the lining (muslin) in relation to the shell or outer fabric. Lightweight outer materials may require heavier interlining to achieve the necessary hand, drape, and recoverability.

"Resilient construction" is a method of manufacture in which outer fabrics and interlining are cut on the bias (an approximately 45° angle). They are held together by a resilient slip-stitch, so that the finished tie can "breathe" or "give", when tied and untied and recover from knotting.

The outer fabric may be cut into two or three pieces so the pattern always runs in the same direction on the tie, and it is then sewn together so that the seams are located in the neckband area under the shirt collar.

After the outer fabrics have been stitched together, the ends are hemmed. Facing or tipping — an extra piece of silk, nylon, rayon or polyester fabric — is added to the back of the ends of the tie. After the seams and tips are pressed into shape, the interlining is slip-stitched to the outer shell with resilient nylon thread. Slip stitching allows the tie to move and "breathe" and still return to its original shape. You may see some excess thread with a tiny knot at the end which will get longer or shorter as the slip stitching tightens and loosens. This is a sign of a well-made tie — do not cut it off!

A bar tack stitch is often added as a finishing touch to the tie, adding a dash of color and neatly fastening the ends of the seams together.

The last manufacturing step is pressing the tie on the reverse side, with care being taken to assure that the edges have a proper roll and are not pressed flat.

A loop label, or sometimes a separate loop in addition to the label, is sewn on the back to allow the small end to be slipped through after tying.

The finished tie should measure 56" to 57" in length. If you are very tall or have a large neck, you might need an extra long tie which measures from 60" to 62".

Neckwear has taken on a wider profile and is designed in a tapered manner, making it possible to tie a smaller knot. The width of most ties will be in the range of $3\frac{1}{2}$" to $4\frac{1}{4}$".

"Ties are the lipstick of a man's wardrobe."

– Source unknown

Choosing Color and Patterns in Ties

The necktie is a personal form of advertising. It communicates your attitude and position. You should choose the patterns of the tie as carefully as you would choose your business card.

Currently, we are experiencing one of the most fascinating periods in the history of men's neckwear. In recent years, the industry has exploded with an unprecedented variety of styles, patterns and textures — adding veritable art to the wardrobe, and expanding choice for the consumer.

Pattern

The old rules of solid tie on patterned shirt and solid shirt with patterned suit are gone — pattern-on-pattern is definitely in. But with this new freedom comes confusion. Which patterns should you wear with what? Here are some suggestions.

The simplest pattern for a tie is, of course, no pattern, i.e., the solid tie. Though at one time considered the staple of any wardrobe, the assortment available today has made it an unnecessary item. If you insist on one or two, make sure the silk has a pattern that at least makes the fabric interesting. A woven grenadine is the most elegant of these solid patterns.

Solid ties are not necessary when wearing even the boldest of stripes. Just make sure that there is spacing between the pattern, allowing the background color of the tie to show. You will see that it will not fight the stripe. The small disconnected "Hèrmes" type patterns are hard to wear with bold stripes.

The paisleys, as well as the fashion-forward geometrics and florals, which have interconnecting patterns, work well with striped shirts. Because the patterns never end, the eye is not confused when looking at the tie on the shirt. These styles will complement the shirts and add interest and variety to your wardrobe.

Your pattern can also make your outfit more or less formal. Polka dots, especially the small ones, are very formal. The club ties are best worn with sport coats. The paisley is more casual and the small geometric more formal.

The most popular of the striped ties is the "Regimental". This tie is of English ancestry. Originally, these ties displayed the colors of the British regiments or clubs of which the wearer was a member. In England the stripes run from high left to low right, but in America it's the opposite. These ties look best on solid shirts or shirts which are perceived as solid, such as very narrow or widely spaced stripes or muted checks. Be careful of these if you are wearing a bold or multi-colored stripe.

Color

Color in ties today has become explosive. It's no longer necessary to wear conservative ties with neat patterns. Geometrics and bright colors in the pattern of the ties lead in fashion. The expanded selection helps you create a new and fresher look for that special shirt.

One guideline to keep in mind when choosing color is to make the tie brighter or deeper in color than the shirt.

A deep rich background color always looks dressier. A deep burgundy is far more elegant than fire engine red, and forest green more elegant than kelly. If you match the background color of the tie to the suit, it becomes a much dressier and conservative ensemble. With a dark suit and a dark tie the light-colored or white shirt is best.

To liven up your outfit, look for vivid color in the pattern of the dark tie. Pure white or bright yellow can add that dash to a dark suit and solid shirt. The strange colors, however, should always be in the pattern — not the background —of the tie.

Try to choose a color which picks up a color of the shirt in the pattern of the tie and have the background of the tie complement the shirt color. For example, on a bright yellow and medium blue striped shirt, a navy tie with bright yellow highlights would be a perfect match.

If the tie does not match the shirt in color, it can be a color that is complementary. For example, on a pink (striped or solid) shirt, a tie with burgundy or helio in the pattern on a navy background would look great. Or the burgundy or helio could be the background color with the pattern bringing in shades of blues and grays.

> *"A well-tied tie is the first serious step in life."*
> – Oscar Wilde

When you wear a white shirt or a colored shirt with a contrasting white collar, try to make sure that your tie has at least a speck of white in it. You will be surprised how much better the outfit will look.

Tying the perfect knot.

With the changing styles in men's collars, came a change in the way most men tie a necktie.

Back in the days of the Duke of Windsor and Cary Grant, the Windsor (also called the Full Windsor), knot was very common. Most collar styles, whether straight, button-down or spread, had wide space at the top of the collar. The large Windsor knot filled this tie space nicely.

The Windsor is now seen mostly on the older generation. In fact, many of these men who were taught to tie in their teens never learned how to tie the newer, smaller knots.

The Half-Windsor, which is not as full a knot as the Windsor, is useful for the widespread collars. It forms an inverted triangle at the throat, filling some of the space designed into the spread collar.

Today's collar styles have less space between the collar points. A tie space of $^1/_4$" or less is common, regardless of the spread of the collar.

For this reason, the most popular knot these days is the four-in-hand. This smaller knot looks better in the narrow tie space of today's collars.

The new ties are designed in a tapered manner, i.e., narrower in the knotting area, making it possible to tie the smaller knot. Some manufacturers have also switched to lighter-weight linings to keep the knots from getting too bulky.

The following are directions for making the two most common knots tied today, The Four-in-Hand and the Half Windsor.

Four-in-Hand

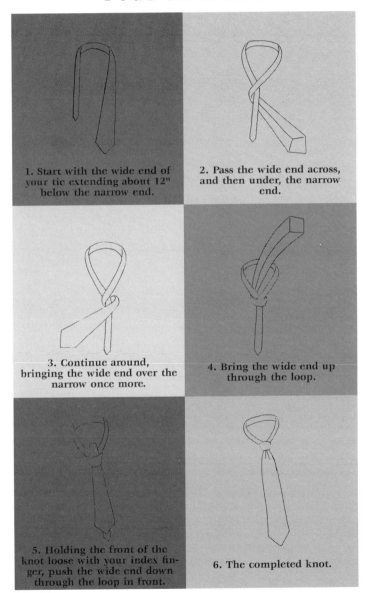

1. Start with the wide end of your tie extending about 12" below the narrow end.

2. Pass the wide end across, and then under, the narrow end.

3. Continue around, bringing the wide end over the narrow once more.

4. Bring the wide end up through the loop.

5. Holding the front of the knot loose with your index finger, push the wide end down through the loop in front.

6. The completed knot.

The Half-Windsor

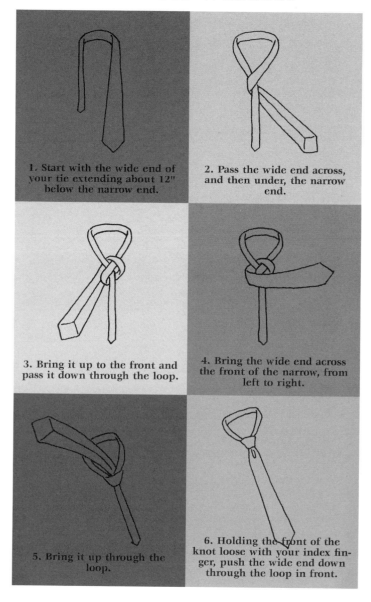

1. Start with the wide end of your tie extending about 12" below the narrow end.

2. Pass the wide end across, and then under, the narrow end.

3. Bring it up to the front and pass it down through the loop.

4. Bring the wide end across the front of the narrow, from left to right.

5. Bring it up through the loop.

6. Holding the front of the knot loose with your index finger, push the wide end down through the loop in front.

Tighten both knots by holding the narrow end and sliding the knot up tight to the collar. When knotted, the tie should meet, but not overlap your belt buckle. The tip should be just where your navel is.

How many ties are enough?

You should have at least two ties per shirt. For the typical business wardrobe, that means about two dozen ties. More would be better, because it would enable you to stretch your shirt and suit collection. But, if you're like most men, you'll probably keep wearing a small number of your favorites. You should, however, try not to wear the same tie more than once per week.

In most cases, each tie should go with more than one shirt. Each tie will look different with each shirt and each shirt will look different with each tie and each combination will make the suit look different and on and on and on.

THE BOW TIE

The black silk bow tie, shaped in either the butterfly or batwing (straight) style, was and is the premier tie for the formal occasion. Other colors are used, usually with a matching cummerbund, but nothing has replaced the black silk beauty. Incidentally, this is the only time a pre-tied bow tie is acceptable.

The selection of other bow ties is as varied as the color combinations and patterns of the standard ties, and they seem to be gaining in popularity. They look great with the classic collar or the button-down, and serve as a real showcase for the shirt.

Knowing how to tie a bow tie will add to your wardrobe options. Let's teach you how.

HOW TO TIE A BOW TIE

Tying a bow tie is not as hard as it looks. In fact, it's as simple as tying your shoelace.

A few secrets:

a) Don't look in the mirror when you're tying, because the mirror reverses the reflection and can confuse you.

b) If your bow tie is the type that can be set for size, set it at least 1" above your neck size to allow room for your collar.

c) Pull the knot tight — if you let it hang loose, the tie will droop.

d) When forming the bow, keep the fold close to the knot or you won't get it tight enough.

e) Pull the bow tight.

f) Use the mirror to straighten the tie and arrange the ends and loops neatly.

The Bow Tie

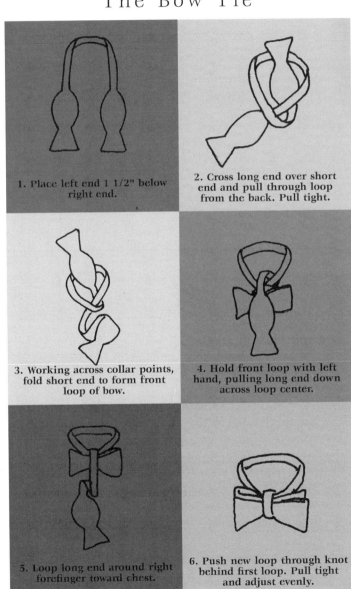

1. Place left end 1 1/2" below right end.

2. Cross long end over short end and pull through loop from the back. Pull tight.

3. Working across collar points, fold short end to form front loop of bow.

4. Hold front loop with left hand, pulling long end down across loop center.

5. Loop long end around right forefinger toward chest.

6. Push new loop through knot behind first loop. Pull tight and adjust evenly.

Helpful Tie Hints:

Q: *How should I take care of my neckties?*

A: A silk tie should always be untied properly. If you pull at the knot, you may damage the silk or tear the lining. Never loosen the tie and take it off over your head. Untie it gently and let the creases hang out overnight.

- Never leave your tie knotted when it is not being worn.
- Have enough of a tie selection so that you don't have to wear the same tie two days running.
- To get rid of creases, hang your tie in the bathroom while showering.
- If you must press your tie, do not touch the tie with an iron; instead, put a cloth over the tie and simply steam gently.
- Don't keep touching the knot during the day. If you do, eventually it will look darker than the rest of the tie.
- If you need to have a tie cleaned, send it to a tie cleaning expert, not just a dry cleaner. (Many dry cleaners do, however, serve as collection points for specialty tie-cleaning and repair services. Of these services, Tiecrafters in New York — the service we use for customers of The Shirt Store — is one of the very best.)

THE BUSINESS SUIT

Fashion may come and go but the basic styling, fabric and construction of a good suit varies little from year to year. That's a good thing, since the suit is probably the most expensive item in most men's wardrobes. Even with the trend to more casual dressing, for most men the suit is the basic uniform of the business world.

"You never get a second chance to make a first impression."

– Will Rogers

Fabric

A good business suit is always made of wool. Like the cotton in your shirt, it has the ability to absorb moisture, keep you cool in the summer and warm in the winter.

Wool is easy to press, wears well, tailors best and resists wrinkling.

Cloth is described by weight per running yard. Spring and summer weight is usually plain weave cloth of seven to nine ounces. Fall and winter weights range from 10 to 13 ounces. Spring, summer and fall cloths tend to have a clear-cut surface with no nap. Winter cloths are usually milled slightly to give a lofty, hairier surface to the cloth.

For year-round business wear, you should choose the moderate or light-weighted cloths (from nine to ten ounces).

The fabric weight you choose should also depend upon your size, the number of suits you have and how often you wear them. The tougher you are on your clothing, the heavier the fabric should be.

Feel the cloth you are considering — you will quickly develop a sense of how smooth a finish you want your suiting cloths to have.

Color and Pattern

Color is the most important choice you make in a suit. Mistakes in pattern and styling might not be noticed if the color is right, for color is what is always seen first. The suit is just a backdrop for the shirt and the tie. It gives you a background on which you paint your own landscape.

The two basic suits every man needs in his business wardrobe are the solid navy (fashion colors ranging from dark blue to midnight blue can also suffice) and solid gray suit. If you have room in your budget, add a muted pattern or stripe in the same basic colors. The fourth color to add is tan — not brown. (For some reason, accessorizing brown suits is still not understood by most men. It's not a good choice for the basic wardrobe.)

In the U.S., suitability of color varies by region. Generally speaking, the farther north and east you go, the darker the colors and the more conservative the styles. Color and pattern get lighter and more relaxed as you travel south and west.

When you are selecting pattern, try to choose a muted one that works well with many different shirts. The bolder the pattern in your suit the more restricted you will be in selecting patterns in your shirts and ties. The pinstripe suit or the muted plaid are perfect choices. They are treated like solid suits when coordinating your shirts and ties.

They are simply interesting fabrics. You can pick up the colors in the pattern and try to match your shirts and ties to bring these colors out.

Style

Unlike the wide range of styles in women's clothing, men's choice in styles is relatively simple. A suit is, basically, either single-breasted or double-breasted.

The single-breasted suit is the cut worn by most businessmen. The natural shoulder has been the standard for years.

Of late, the double breasted suit has been making a comeback. "Everyone, no matter what their size, looks good in it. Even a big man can look 20 lbs. thinner in a well fitted double-breasted suit," says Sonny Catania, a custom tailor in New York.

He goes on to say, "A suit should have expression. Expression is a quality that is indefinable, just as a beautiful woman is indefinable. You know that a suit has expression when you see it. It's a simplicity of style, quality of construction, of fabric and fit which combine to give a suit a look which makes it uniquely yours. You are not covered, you are dressed.

"It looks good on you ...it fits well...it looks like you...it has Expression!"

Helpful Hint

When you get your suits tailored, ask for swatches of the fabrics. Put them in your wallet and bring them out when you are buying your shirts and ties. It will take some of the guesswork out of shopping.

Tailoring

There are basically three types of tailoring available in suits: custom-tailored, made-to-measure or off-the-rack. Usually your choice is determined by your wallet and your patience.

Custom

Because a custom-made suit is hand-made in its entirety, it is the most expensive suit you can buy. The garment is literally constructed on your body. There are many fitting sessions and there are as many hand-sewing operations as the tailor deems necessary. The final result is a garment of matchless quality and fit.

Made-To-Measure

In contrast to the custom suit, a made-to-measure suit has less hand labor and more machine sewing. There are fewer fittings and alterations, but the resulting garment is still of excellent quality — at a more affordable cost.

Off-the-rack

The stock suit has the broadest range in quality of construction and fabric. Consequently, it also has the broadest range of cost. A stock suit can cost as little as $100, or as much as $2,000.

They are called stock suits because they are cut for the "average" man. For example, all size 44's will have 44" chests, 38" waists and 46" hips. These same proportions will hold true for all 42's, 40's, 38's, etc. This conformity of proportion gives continuity to the manufacturing process, resulting in lower costs. The cost of a stock suit rises when more expensive fabrics are used and when features are added that require hand labor.

TAILORING DETAILS
Jackets

Buttons should be sewn on firmly. Look for buttons that are cross-stitched—they will hold better.

Pockets — Outer pockets come in two varieties: patch or inset. Patch means that the entire pocket is attached to the suit, and all sides are visible. The inset pocket is hidden except for the pocket opening or flap. More formal business suits should always have inset pockets.

There should be at least one or two inside breast pockets. Some suits have more. Look for the number that makes you comfortable.

Linings should be made from a smooth, silky material so that the jacket slides easily over the shirt. The tighter the stitching in the lining, the better.

Sleeve Length

When making a suit jacket, the tailor should measure up from the break of the wrist, depending on how much cuff the wearer wants to show out of his suit jacket. For example, if you want to show $1/2$" of cuff, the jacket should end $1/2$" above the break of the wrist.

It is proper to show at least $1/2$" of cuff at the wrist. Caution: some tailors use the thumb as a guide for the length of the suit jacket — they start at the tip of the thumb and measure up five inches. However, thumbs come in all sizes and shapes. You will get a nicer finish if you forget the thumb and stick to the break of the wrist and up!

Vents are the only detail acceptable on a suit back. They are, however, not a necessity. Sometimes no vent or a center vent provides a longer elegant line. The center vent, however, is not a good detail for the man with the large seat. Side vents are more desirable for a man who has a habit of keeping his hands in his pockets.

Trousers

At one time, cuffs on trousers were considered casual. They originated in England when a "gentleman" turned up the bottoms of his trousers for walks in the country, so his pant legs would not get muddy. In town, the "gentleman" always rode in a carriage, so the turned up cuffs were not necessary.

Today's rules of cuffs or no cuffs are not absolute. It really is up to the individual. Pleated pants usually are styled with cuffs to add weight and drape to the fabric. Trousers styled without pleats tend to be styled without cuffs.

Trouser length should extend past the shoe line. In fact, the trouser should cover half of the shoe in front and drop a little below the top of the shoe in the back. Your socks should never show unless you are seated.

How Many Suits Are Enough?

If you wear a suit every business day, three suits is the minimum you should have. That will give them time to "hang out" and regain their shape between wearings. No suit should be worn day after day if you want to look your best. Five suits, or more, would of course be better. And it's a good idea to have at least two suits in your favorite basic color.

Helpful Suit Hints:

Q: *How should I take care of my suits?*

A: Be sure to hang up your suit after each wearing. Use a wooden suit hanger to help bring it back into shape. Air it out before putting it into the confines of your closet.

- Don't leave the pockets full — empty them after each use.
- Do not clean your suit unless it is dirty. If it needs pressing, just have it pressed. Cleaning will reduce the life of the garment.

CUFF LINKS

When the modern cuff emerged in the middle of the 19th century, and starch became popular to make the cuffs more formal, it became too difficult to get buttons through the stiff material. So cuff links, as we know them today, were born. They were used by men and women alike, and almost everyone wore them until the 1920's, when shirts became more casual and cuffs were no longer starched. The advent of the sport shirt brought the decline of the cuff link, but it remained in use for formal business and evening wear.

Today, more and more men are wearing cuff links to the office as well as in the evenings, and manufacturers are constantly introducing new designs. In fact, cuff links are growing in popularity among collectors.

In the January 1994 issue of its quarterly publication, "The Link", the National Cuff Link Society answered the question, "Why do people wear cuff links?" and pointed out that the need to be "in vogue" was, interestingly, not one of the reasons. Here, based on numerous polls, are the main reasons cited for wearing cuff links:

- Cuff links allow me to distinguish myself from the crowd.
- They show that I care about my appearance.
- Various styles, colors and sizes of cuff links allow me to express my mood.
- Cuff links allow me to show my success on my sleeve.
- Wearing them allows me to display my collection.
- They provide the formal look that I prefer in business.
- Cuff links complement my taste in clothing and accessories.

Analyzing the above findings, Mr. Eugene Klompus, president of the National Cuff Link Society, determined that "the composite cuff link wearer is discriminating, proud, and expressive. Perhaps the most common characteristic of all the respondents was an almost palpable self-confidence."

Susan Jonas and Marilyn Nissenson, in their book "Cuff Links", published by Harry N. Abrams, point out:

"Cuff links are utilitarian objects, so the options for design are finite. They have to fit through a hole of a relatively certain size. They can't bang into things when the wearer is moving around. They have to slide into the jacket sleeve, so they can't protrude too far. And yet people are endlessly inventive." There have been cuff links made of all kinds of metals, set with gems, inlaid, painted — in all sorts of shapes — and even cuff links made of human hair.

Modern cuff links can be found in almost all men's stores, and a look in any antique shop will turn up several examples of Victorian cuff links. As Ms. Nissenson says, "in their own small way [cuff links] are a piece of social and sartorial history."

The newest trend in cufflinks is the knotted silk links. They are seen in the most conservative settings and they are great to throw in your suitcase for the last-minute business trip. They come in a wide assortment of colors and can be matched to the colors of the tie, shirt or suit. They are inexpensive so most wardrobes can afford to have a wide assortment. (They are very difficult to get in while you are wearing the shirt. It's easiest if you put them on before you put on the shirt — they are elasticized and will stretch enough for your hand to go through.)

OTHER JEWELRY

Other than cuff links, the only jewelry that is acceptable is the collar pin or bar, the tie pin or bar, your watch and, of course, your wedding ring!

BELTS

Good leather is the rule for the business belt. Plain black is the one belt everyone needs. A neat, simple metal buckle is best. Belts should be no wider than $1^{1}/_{4}$" for a business suit. As your suit wardrobe grows, add more belts. The belt should blend with the suit. It should not be a focal point. It is used to hold up your trousers, not to make a fashion statement. If your belt is noticed, it is too flashy or too worn.

SOCKS

If you are starting your wardrobe, buy black socks which fit over-the-calf, preferably cotton or cotton blend. Cotton socks are cooler and are easily washed. As your wardrobe grows, so should your colors: brown, blue, gray, navy, maroon, etc. — but always dark.

SHOES

Men's shoe styles do not change much from year to year, so it pays to invest in a well-made, long-lasting shoe that will offer years of comfort and pleasure.

Lace-up shoes

Because of its versatility, the plain-toe oxford in black is the one indispensible shoe for every business wardrobe. Whether it is a power breakfast, business lunch or formal dinner, the black, plain-toed oxford is correct footwear. Though more limited in use, a wing-tip oxford is also an essential component to the business wardrobe.

Slip-on shoes

Though frowned upon by the older, more conservative, lace-up generation, slip-ons are now acceptable for business, and for formal and casual occasions. Every man should have at least one pair of loafers, be they tassel loafers from Gucci or penny loafers from Land's End.

How many

For the start-up business wardrobe you need a minimum of two pairs of good black shoes, one of which must be a plain-toed oxford. The second pair could be a wing-tip oxford or a business-like plain slip on. The third shoe should be a loafer, brown or cordovan in color.

As your wardrobe expands, so should your choice of shoes. This will enable you to rotate the shoes you wear, prolonging their life and giving you a different look. Most important, always wear newly polished shoes, and never wear a shoe that looks run-down.

SUSPENDERS

Suspenders ("braces" in England) are strips of material, usually silk or elastic, worn over the shoulders and attached to the front and back of the trousers.

They are available with clips or with buttons. The proper finish for the business suit is buttons.

It's nice to wear a suspender that complements the tie. It should not match in exact pattern, like a cummerbund and bow tie set. It should just be complementing patterns and colors.

If you wear suspenders, you should not wear a belt. One, not both, is proper.

POCKET SQUARES

The pocket square is not a necessary item in a man's wardrobe. It is, however, one of the most dashing accessories that the well-dressed man can add. This small splash of color worn in the suit breast pocket can be the finishing touch to an outfit.

Pocket squares can be of white cotton, linen or silk. The silks can be colored solids or patterns. White silk is usually worn for formal occasions, while white cotton, white linen, or colored silks are acceptable in both casual and dress situations. The pattern or color should complement the tie, but does not have to match. We encourage the mixing of pattern and color to add interest to the wardrobe.

"It has long been an axiom of mine that the little things are infinitely the most important."

– *Source unknown*

104

Placement in the pocket should be a fluid motion. The fabric should not be folded and pressed, but, rather, placed ends down or up to show the natural edges or fullness of the square.

Simply pick up the square from the very center, letting the points hang down. Put it in your pocket with the points facing either up or down, for two different looks. Adjust the silk slightly, if you wish, but the casual, haphazard look is a good one.

Less popular, and far more conservative, is the formal multi-pointed fold. This fold works better with cotton or linen handkerchiefs. It is more complicated than the others and, in our opinion, lacks the dash and style of the other two looks. There is a diagram on the next page for those who wish to try:

The Pocket Square

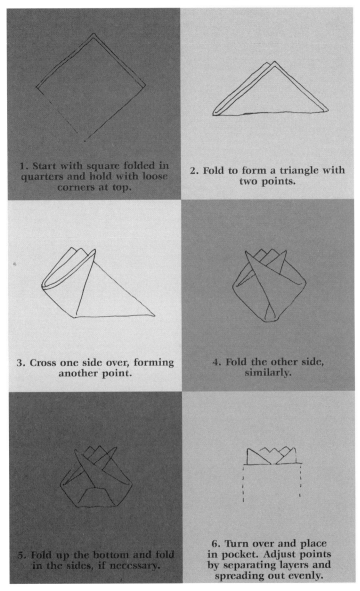

1. Start with square folded in quarters and hold with loose corners at top.

2. Fold to form a triangle with two points.

3. Cross one side over, forming another point.

4. Fold the other side, similarly.

5. Fold up the bottom and fold in the sides, if necessary.

6. Turn over and place in pocket. Adjust points by separating layers and spreading out evenly.

Conclusion

To repeat:

Your shirt should subtly reflect who and what you are, as part of a whole ensemble that says "this man is worth listening to." The ability to make this kind of impact is not innate, it is learned. I hope this book has helped.

"The sense of being perfectly well-dressed gives a feeling of inward tranquility which religion is power-less to bestow."

–Ralph Waldo Emerson